This Book
Belongs To

Also by William C. Ketchum, Jr.

Early Potters and Potteries of New York State (1970)

The Pottery and Porcelain Collectors Handbook (1971)

American Basketry and Woodenware (1974)

A Treasury of American Bottles (1975)

Hooked Rugs (1976)

The Family Treasury of Antiques (1978)

The Catalogue of American Antiques (1977, 1980, 1984)

The Catalogue of American Collectibles (1979, 1984)

Collecting American Craft Antiques (1980)

Auction (1980)

Western Memorabilia (1980)

Toys and Games (Smithsonian Illustrated Library of Antiques) (1981)

Furniture, Vol. II (Smithsonian Illustrated Library of Antiques) (1981)

The Catalogue of World Antiques (1981)

Boxes (Smithsonian Illustrated Library of Antiques) (1982)

American Furniture, Cupboards, Chests and Related Pieces (1982)

Pottery and Porcelain (1983)

American Folk Art of the Twentieth Century (1983)

Collecting Bottles for Fun and Profit (1985)

Collecting Toys for Fun and Profit (1985)

Collecting Sporting Memorabilia for Fun and Profit (1985)

Collecting the 40's and 50's for Fun and Profit (1985)

All American Folk Art and Crafts (1986)

American Country Pottery

AMERICAN · COUNTRY · POTTERY

Yellowware and Spongeware

by WILLIAM C. KETCHUM, JR.

With photographs by Schecter Lee

ALFRED A. KNOPF   *New York*   1987

THIS IS A BORZOI BOOK
PUBLISHED BY ALFRED A. KNOPF, INC.

Library of Congress Cataloging-in-Publication Data

Ketchum, William C., [date]
American country pottery.

Bibliography: p.
1. Yellowware—United States.   2. Sponged ware—
United States.   3. Pottery—19th century—United
States.   4. Pottery—20th century—United States.
I. Title.
NK4340.Y44K48   1987   738.3′0973   87-45132
ISBN 0-394-75244-9

Manufactured in Japan

First Edition

CONTENTS

Introduction   3

The Manufacture of Yellowware and Spongeware   7

Yellowware Manufacturers   13

Yellowware Forms   31

Spongeware Manufacturers   89

Spongeware Forms   95

Appendix: A List of Spongeware and Yellowware Makers   139

Bibliography   147

American Country Pottery

Introduction

Nostalgia for an earlier and supposedly better time is a common preoccupation of modern life, and one of the central facets of this myth is the kitchen. Here it was that the mother, often assisted by grandmother, aunts, daughters, and all the rest of the extended family (female only, of course), met to create those remarkable meals which became the subject of Norman Rockwell magazine covers and the cause of an alarming increase in obesity, heart failure, and other sundry ills of our first consumer society.

As we seek now a connection to those less hurried times, we adorn our homes with the wooden bowls, tinware, and baskets which were the commonplaces of those days. And among these wares none are more typical or more appropriate than the simple yellow- and spongeware cooking and serving utensils that once graced the shelves of every country and city cupboard.

The first of the legendary *Fannie Farmer Cookbooks*, published in 1896, contained an illustration of proper techniques for stirring and beating cake batter. The bowl recommended for this chore was a heavy one of banded yellowware. Forty years later advertisements in such popular home magazines as *Ladies Home Journal* and *The Saturday Evening Post* still featured smiling matrons with their hands buried deep within similar vessels. In most cases the illustrated scene would also feature a sponged pitcher, pie plates, and perhaps a storage crock or hanging salt container. All would be of yellow- or spongeware. In fact, until the post–World War II advent of plastics, these wares were regarded as a household necessity not only in the kitchen but in the pantry, bath, and bedroom as well.

An early writer for the universally respected *Godey's Lady's Book* advised her readers that

for the bath we strongly recommend a toilet set in ironstone, perhaps one of those with the gaily mottled surfaces which are so much in vogue now. These are strong and durable, and most important for health's sake, easily and thoroughly cleaned. . . .

The durability of yellowware and spongeware was certainly a factor in their favor. Redware utensils had always been considered fragile as well as dangerous, due to their lead-based glaze. The frequent references to yellowwares as "fireproof" or as "oven ware" spoke eloquently of their ability to survive in the daily grind of homemaking. Since most spongeware was of stoneware or yellowware clay, it too had this virtue.

Another factor which commended these ceramics to the general market was their simple forms and earthy colors. In this sense they are not unlike the peasant wares of Europe, the faience and the blue-decorated stonewares of the Rhine Valley. While the housewife might dream of porcelain and adorn her Sunday table with transfer-printed whitewares from Staffordshire or the American Staffordshire of East Liverpool, she spent most of her time in the kitchen with vessels whose hues reminded her of the blue of the Ohio sky and the rich yellow of ripening Missouri corn. That such preferences have not changed all that much is evidenced not only by current collector interest in older examples but also by the fact that both yellowware and sponge have continued to be made right down to the present day.

True, some have referred to these as "transitional ceramics," which served to bridge the gap between early hand-thrown redware and stoneware and the industrially made white earthenwares which dominate the contemporary table. To a certain extent this generalization is correct, though it is doubtful that early manufacturers, especially of yellowware, saw things in this light.

Certainly, David Henderson of Jersey City was aiming higher. He imported English potters skilled in the production of porcelain and white earthenwares, and his molds were those used abroad in the manufacture of those wares. And the 1841 Pittsburgh Business Directory had this to say of James Bennett, long regarded as one of the seminal figures in the history of American yellowware: "In this town [East Liverpool] . . . there is the manufactory (now in successful operation) of Porcelain which is carried on by Mr Bennett, a regular manufacturer, from Staffordshire, England. . . ." Of course, Bennett was not making porcelain. In the same publication he is referred to at a different point as a "Queensware" manufacturer, a term often, though inaccurately, used to describe yellowware.

The point, however, is that American potters in most cases did not view the making of yellowware as an end in itself. They saw the clay as a ductile, easily cast material, which might with further refinement approximate the pure white earth that they sought. Time and circumstances proved them wrong, though; and within a few years yellowware had retreated from its brief foray into the dining room and parlor. Henceforth, its destiny was more humble—to be the handmaid of the kitchen crew.

Spongewares had a somewhat different history, though in the end the result was the same. Here decoration, not clay was the key, and several earths might be used for the body. The earliest employed in this country was probably whiteware, since there seems to be a link between sponge and the more delicate spatterware which was produced, almost exclusively for export, in England during the eighteenth and early nineteenth centuries. At least one American manufacturer, Edwin Bennett of Baltimore, is known to have made spatterware; and since he also produced marked spongeware, it is not surprising to learn that the same ironstone china body was used for both.

Another link is with Rockingham which, in this country, was produced by glazing a yellowware body with brown slip. As much later American spongeware employed a yellow clay body, it is reasonable to assume a connection between the wares.

However, better than 50 percent of existent spongeware is based on a coarse stoneware body, usually first covered with the opaque white slip referred to as Bristol from its believed city of origin. These pieces are late—few date prior to 1900—and in most instances the bodies are heavy and the decoration crude, reflecting less the lack of skill of the workmen than the inherent difficulties of working with this clay. Stoneware can be cast. Henderson produced some splendid bodies in the 1830s, but the task is not an easy one. In any case, sponged stoneware vessels tend to be less complex. Whereas one will find blue-sponged white earthenware plates, covered sugars, and gravy boats, sponge-decorated stoneware is confined primarily to such basics as pitchers, bowls, and water coolers.

These wares were less transitional than specialized. In days when cooking was done on wood or coal ranges and both solids and liquids in bulk were handled on a daily basis, it was necessary that household utensils be long-lasting. In fact, only the development of modern conveniences such as the electric stove, the microwave oven, and the refrigerator wholly eliminated the need for their strength and durability.

The large quantity of advertising or promotional ware among sponge and yellowware vessels indicates that nineteenth- and twentieth-century promoters clearly recognized that one of the best ways to reach the customer was through his or her stomach. Selling a pound of butter in a spongeware crock bearing a stenciled message proclaiming the virtues of "Hazel, Extra Creamery Butter" was a surefire sales promoter. Every time the piece was reused (because you can be sure it was not thrown away), the advertiser's message reappeared. More subtle merchants placed the promotional logo in the bottom of a bowl, so that each time the housewife prepared to bake a cake or stir up a bit of soup, she came face to face with "Hazel Foods Are Pure," or, "We Appreciate Your Business: Edgar Fair Store."

These advertisers and the makers of yellowware and spongeware knew their markets. They were going directly to those, the women of the house, who made the decisions both as to what to buy and where to buy it. That same simple and direct appeal is reflected in the attraction which so many collectors feel for these utilitarian ceramics.

The Manufacture of
Yellowware and Spongeware

As they were, for the most part, intended to be low-cost, mass-produced wares, yellowware and spongeware were manufactured in ways that were both rapid and inexpensive. This generally meant the use of molds and the making of many very similar pieces, which were distinguished one from the other by their decoration. Since yellowware was the more widely made, it is appropriate to deal with this first.

Yellowware

In general, the term "yellowware" is applied to a ceramic body which fires to a yellowish hue—though this may vary from a dark golden yellow to an extremely pale shade, depending upon both the nature of the clay employed and the temperature at which it is fired. Yellow firing clays are found widely throughout much of the United States, with major sources located in New Jersey and Ohio.

The earth is a particularly ductile one, that is, when mixed with water to produce a slip it flows easily and lends itself to casting. It is also a finer-grained clay than either redware or stoneware clay, and considerably less dense and vitreous than the latter. On the other hand, it fires at around 2,200 degrees to a hard, durable body, which particularly lends itself to use in baking and other purposes requiring constant exposure to high temperatures. This, of course, is one of the reasons that yellowware, often referred to as "yellow baking ware" or "fireproof ware," found its way into the kitchen.

Except in rare cases, such as flowerpots or chemical wares, yellowware is glazed with a clear glaze, either lead- or alkaline-based. Both finishes impart a shiny, glasslike effect, which greatly enhances the natural yellow hue of the ware. However, due to the toxic quality of the glaze, lead was soon abandoned in favor of a more benign alkaline glaze generally consisting of some mixture of kaolin, ground flint, and white lead.

While yellowware is customarily mold-cast, it may be turned on a wheel or drape-molded. Early mixing bowls were often shaped on the potter's wheel, and these were then referred to in price lists as "turned" or "plain," to distinguish them from cast bowls. Pie plates were formed over a round drape mold identical to that used in producing similar redware examples.

Cast or molded pieces were produced with the use of shaped molds, usually of plaster (as that absorbed water, expediting the process), though they might be of baked clay. The technique was known as slip casting, and involved the pouring of liquid slip into the hollow mold. This was allowed to sit until a suitable thickness had dried and adhered to the mold wall; the excess was then poured off. Since the technique was necessarily somewhat arbitrary, the walls of similar pitchers, teapots, and so on will vary substantially in thickness depending on the technique and whim of the molder.

In most instances, yellowware was fired twice. The first or "bisque" firing was at maximum temperature and served to vitrify the body. A second or "gloss" firing at a lower temperature served to fix whatever decoration and glaze might have been applied. While most yellowware is simply clear-glazed, decoration is also common. Most often seen are horizontal bands of color, typically white, brown, or blue. These are applied through use of a slip cup, a small vessel with one or more spouts extending from it somewhat in the manner of a teapot. The decorator would fill the slip cup with slip—a mixture of fine clay, water, and a coloring agent—and then dribble it onto the surface of the ware as the piece was turned on a potter's wheel.

As may be seen from the illustrations, banding may vary greatly, from a single stripe of a single hue to several of contrasting colors. Moreover, wide, usually white, bands were sometimes enhanced by the application of an acidic mixture, which might consist variously of tobacco juice, turpentine, clay slip, and even stale urine. When dropped onto an unfired or "green" body, this concoction would ramify into various dendritic or "treelike" forms. A skillful artisan could pour the liquid in such a way as to create designs which collectors now refer to as seaweed, thistle, earthworm, feather, pinetree, cat's eye, and so on. Referred to as Mocha or Moco decoration, due to its fancied similarity to the cut and polished surface of the gemstone moss agate found chiefly at Mocha in the Near East, this decoration was applied primarily to white earthenware bodies. Its application to yellowware is relatively late; moreover, the majority of such pieces appear to be of English origin. However, there is no doubt that the technique was employed here. It is thought that Edwin Bennett·of Baltimore made Mocha ware, and an 1880s catalogue issued by the C. C. Thompson & Company pottery of East Liverpool, Ohio, illustrates Mocha-decorated mixing bowls and chamberpots.

Some have argued that the term Mocha decoration (as with Rockingham, we are dealing here with a decoration, not a ware such as stoneware or yellowware) should apply only to a branching tree-like design on a muddy yellow or burnt orange ground, since this is the appearance of the Mocha stone or Moss Agate for which it is named. This, however, is an unnecessarily pedantic approach. Other designs such as seaweed on a blue ground and earthworm on white are termed Mocha by both manufacturers and collectors.

All or most of a yellowware body might also be covered with colored slip. The Pacific Clay Manufacturing Company of Riverside, California, produced bowls completely covered with streaky combinations of red, brown, green, and black glazes. There are also late nineteenth-century pitchers and teapots attributed to the Globe Pottery of East Liverpool, which have embossed decoration of a floral nature heavily slipped in red, blue, green, brown, and white. Such wares are technically yellow-bodied, yet they are of less interest to many collectors than are more typical forms. Another often yellow-bodied ware is Rockingham, which will be discussed in detail below.

Much yellowware was molded for decoration as well as for form. Such embellishment ranges from simple raised gridwork, embossed lines, and scalloped rims to the remarkably complex surfaces of the fine early pitchers and mugs made at the New Jersey potteries in the 1820–40 period. In the creation of such pieces, the potter would often combine casting with freehand work, involving the application of separately shaped elements such as press-molded flowers or berries, human and animal masks, and tendrils of strained clay—referred to in the trade as "cole slaw." Such elaboration was not characteristic of the field as a whole. Most yellowware was simply formed and simply decorated.

Moreover, with the passage of time and the introduction of mass-production techniques, the ware as a whole became plainer. This, of course, is not offered as a criticism. It is simply a fact; many collectors find the straightforward and almost naive quality of late nineteenth- and twentieth-century yellowware its most charming characteristic.

Since it was intended as a kitchenware, the yellow-bodied ceramic was, particularly after 1900, frequently produced in matching sets which would be identical in embossing or slip decoration. An apt example would be the ware with fluted lower body and a single white slip band between two of brown that was produced by the Red Wing, Minnesota, Potteries during the 1930s and 1940s. Among the matching pieces to be found are mixing bowls, casseroles, pie plates, pitchers, cookie and beater jars. Needless to say, the prospect of a complete and matching set whets the chase for many enthusiasts.

Spongeware

Unlike yellowware, spongeware is defined not by its clay body but by its decoration. In fact, the body may vary from stoneware, perhaps the most common, through yellowware, to an inexpensive and rather coarse white earthenware. What unites these disparate bodies is their decoration: a sponged, or, as it was often termed in makers' catalogues, "mottled" surface.

The manufacture of the body was, however, similar to that employed with yellowware. Though occasionally hand-thrown, the ware was generally cast in molds. These might be either plain-shape molds or cut so as to provide embossed decoration. Particularly where stoneware clay was used, embossed decoration was simple and rather crude in appearance. This reflected the fact that the earth was not only coarser and less refined but also lacked the ductility of the yellow clay. It could not be as easily cast, and the potter was forced to work with less complex forms. Where, as in Red Wing, Minnesota, the same molds were used for both yellow-bodied and stone-bodied spongeware, the clay was specially prepared.

Another characteristic separating spongeware from yellowware is the period during which it was made. While the latter was well established as a ceramic type in this country by the 1830s, American spongeware did not appear in any quantity until the turn of the century. Prior to that time, there were several related wares. Most similar was Rockingham, which was characterized by a streaky brown glaze generally applied over a yellow clay body. When properly done, the result was a surface predominantly in some shade of brown but with yellow areas left exposed to create an effect very like that of tortoise shell, a term used alternatively for the ware. The contrast between the brown glaze and the clay body was most effective when the earth used was yellowware, and some have argued that Rockingham should be simply classified by its body as a yellowware. Of course, technically that might be true, but life is seldom so simple.

In the first place, Rockingham as understood by nineteenth-century potters (and their terminology should govern, rather than words applied years later by collectors) included not only yellow-bodied ware but also that made on a white earthen body in the eighteenth century and the extremely common nineteenth-century "Rockingham," which consisted of a stoneware body dipped completely in a brown manganese slip. While this last might more properly be called brownware, as Ramsay categorized it in *American Potters and Pottery*, it was unquestionably advertised and sold by its makers as Rockingham.

It is not unreasonable to suspect that Rockingham was a forerunner of spongeware, but it is also clear that the appearance of the two wares when seen from their most typical examples is different. Where Rockingham and the closely related Flint Enamel show a streaky surface, spongeware evidences a splotched effect with a much larger area of the body remaining exposed and the color for the most part running very little. Earlier Rockingham and twentieth-century spongeware show these differences quite clearly, but there are many transitional pieces over which reasonable collectors may differ. This is particularly evident in the brown-glazed pie plates, bowls, and bakers of the 1875–1900 period. These, of course, are of a yellow clay.

On the other hand, there is some blue-sponged white earthenware of quite early date. Examples traceable to kilns in New Jersey, Pennsylvania, and Ohio have been found, and all are of white earthenware, reflecting the fact that this ware was a by-product of the growing production of this ceramic during the period 1850 to 1870.

By the time, though, that spongeware was being made in substantial quantity, it was coming from potteries which utilized stoneware and yellowware clays. As a consequence, almost all circa 1880–1940 ware is of one or the other of these bodies. Moreover, these pieces are strictly utilitarian in nature: pitchers, mixing bowls, crocks, jars, custard cups, and other items which would be at home in the kitchen or the chambers, slop jars, and pitcher and bowl sets employed in bedroom and bath.

Spongeware is occasionally confused with other ceramic types. Chief among these is a ware which has come to be known as spatter. This is a body, usually of white earthenware, which has been sprinkled or "spattered" with tiny, more or less uniform dots of color. Such a pattern may cover the entire surface in one or several colors or may frame a reserve in which hand-painted decoration or a transfer-printed design appears.

Another related type has been termed "cut sponge-stamped ware," in the belief that it was decorated by use of pictorial stamps cut from sponge or a similar porous material. Such stamps, in various forms such as stars, crosses, diamonds, florets, and leaflets, would be dipped in color, then applied to the unglazed whiteware surface in order to create different decorative patterns.

Upon examining examples of the above two forms (see illustrations 111 and 112, page 137), the reader will quickly see that both are clearly distinguishable from what has become known as spongeware. Nor are they the subject of this book.

It should also be noted that all of the terms used here, "spongeware," "spatter," and "cut sponge-stamped ware," have been created by collectors and antiques dealers for their convenience. They were not used by the potters who created the wares. Indeed, except for the term "mottled," applied to spongeware, we really do not know what any of these were called by their makers. The term "dipt ware" occurs frequently in early records and in price lists, but we cannot be sure to which, if any, of the above it was applied.

However, it is not difficult to recognize spongeware, though the sponging employed may vary from piece to piece. Some examples show a patterned surface with joined oblongs of color, dubbed "chicken wire" by some collectors. Others are decorated with randomly placed dots or blotches, which may be combined with solid bands similar to those found on yellowware. In yet other instances the decoration will assume a netlike form, or will be arranged in horizontal rows indicating the repetition of a single motif.

Though much of this decoration is random, most pieces do show repeats of a single shape—triangle, "L," "T," or circle—indicating that the decorator applied a color-soaked stamp again and again to the surface, probably as the vessel was turned. The blurred and often indefinite forms left would support the idea that the applicator was a bit of cut sponge or some other soft and absorbent material. Interestingly enough, in almost all cases the same-shaped applicator appears to have been used, even though more than one color was applied to the ceramic body. These variations may be readily seen in illustration 69 (page 108), in the mixing bowl on the left.

A few later sponged pieces also show the use of gilding, usually in the form of fine lines running about the rims of cups or the covers and handles of casseroles. This appears to have been applied after glazing and firing, and it has often worn off over the years. In the case of a yellow clay body, the sponging is applied directly to the raw surface, then the entire piece is given a clear glaze. This technique was also employed with a stoneware body, especially with earlier pieces. However, in most cases stoneware was first coated with an opaque white slip termed "Bristol" for the town in England where it originated. Decorating was then done on the slip surface, and the whole piece was either salt-glazed or covered with a clear alkaline glaze.

Whatever the technique employed, spongeware usually shows a charmingly random and "folky" decoration, with few pieces alike. It is this variation, almost to the point of eccentricity, that many collectors find so appealing.

Yellowware Manufacturers

The earliest reference to an American yellowware maker appears in the December 2, 1797, issue of the *Rising Sun*, a weekly newspaper published at Kingston, New York. This notice, posted by Stephen Bonnet, announced that "A new manufactory of common and yellow WARE, such as was never made in this country before, has been established at Tivoli, near Red Hook, under the name of Tivoli Ware. . . ."

Tivoli, a tiny Hudson Valley community over a hundred miles north of New York City, seems a most unlikely place to serve as the cradle of what came to be such an important industry. Nevertheless, the pottery did operate, at least for a while. Another advertisement, this one in Greenleaf's *New York Daily Advertiser* for May 12, 1798, proclaimed the manufacture of "Queens Ware," a term often used in reference to the yellow-bodied ware; and a further notice of the availability of "refuse ware" or seconds clearly indicates that the kiln was in operation. However, nothing more is known of this works, and no pieces traceable to it have been uncovered.

It is important to note, though, that the earliest references to English yellowware production date only to the 1780s, indicating that the technology necessary to manufacture this pottery arrived here rather quickly.

Another early but obscure reference is to Captain John Mullowny of Philadelphia, who established the Washington Pottery in 1809 and advertised "yellow" pitchers, tea, and coffee-pots until 1816. Mullowny was not a potter, and the kiln in which he installed his business had previously been used to make redware; however, his importation of several highly trained English craftsmen supports the supposition that he made yellowware.

It was over twenty years later that the first successful manufactory was opened. This was located in New Jersey, and that state along with Ohio and Maryland became the focus of the industry.

New Jersey

In 1824 David Henderson, a native of Scotland and a highly successful entrepreneur, whose interests included printing and iron mines, took over the inactive shops of the Jersey Pottery and Porcelain Works in an attempt to manufacture porcelain. Ware was made and distributed to prospective customers, meeting with some favor, as can be seen from the following advertisement in the *Utica* (New York) *Sentinel* of July 18, 1826:

> The subscribers respectfully inform the lovers of Domestic Manufactures that they can by calling at their store be gratified with examining specimens of American China (equal to French Porcelain) manufactured at the works of the New Jersey Porcelain Co. . . . Field & Clark.

However, the business failed; and on September 29, 1828, Henderson purchased the firm's assets, eliminating his former partner, one George Dummer. He immediately set about utilizing the equipment in the making of molded stoneware and yellowware.

The pieces made in this factory over the next fifteen years or so are generally regarded as the finest yellowware ever produced in this country. The employment of skilled modelers such as Daniel Greatbach to create highly detailed molds similar to those used in England to manufacture porcelain and fine earthenwares made yellowware for a brief period the "American porcelain."

In September of 1830 the firm received a silver medal from Philadelphia's Franklin Institute, and only a month later New York's American Institute honored it with a First Premium for its "superior stone, flint and cane colored earthenware. . . ."

The company, which had been known initially as D. & J. Henderson, reflecting the interests of a brother whose first name was James, was incorporated in 1833 as the American Pottery Manufacturing Company, usually referred to as the American Pottery. Its works were at the corner of Warren and Essex streets in Jersey City. Marked examples, including various pitchers as well as utilitarian wares such as nappies, bakers, and plates, are available.

In 1839, the American Pottery produced the first American transfer-printed white earthenware; and thereafter the firm concentrated on whitewares rather than yellowware. David Henderson became involved with iron mining in the Adirondacks of New York State and was accidentally killed near Tahawus in September 1845 when a hunting companion's pistol misfired. He is buried in Albany Rural Cemetery.

The reputation of the Henderson firm rested primarily on the quality of the craftsmen employed, and these read like a *Who's Who* of American ceramics. Besides the previously mentioned Greatbach, there was James Bennett, who established the first yellowware factory at East Liverpool, Ohio; Thomas Locker, William Coxon, Benjamin Brunt, William Bloor, and James Carr, all of whom later owned their own potteries.

By the time that the American Pottery had ceased to make yellowware, several other New Jersey firms had become active in the field. One of the first was that of the English potter John Hancock, who opened a pottery at South Amboy in 1828. The following year with his brother William he began to make yellowware, continuing until 1840 when he, like so many others, "went west" to work at potteries in Louisville, Kentucky, and East Liverpool.

In 1849, Hancock's old shop in South Amboy was purchased by the Manhattan merchant Abraham Cadmus. Now termed the Congress Pottery, it was used until the owner's death in 1854 for the making of yellowware and Rockingham. It is thought that Daniel Greatbach may have modeled some of the more spectacular pieces created here such as the hound-handled pitchers and a mantel ornament in the form of a recumbent calf. Among the other pieces associated with this kiln are batter pitchers, spittoons, and humidors.

Another well-known South Amboy factory was the Swan Hill Pottery, opened in 1849 by Enoch Moore and a man named Sparks. By 1850, the proprietors were Edward Hanks and Charles Fish, and they were the first to mark their yellowware with the logo of a swan, a mark long associated with the kiln. However, this too was a brief venture. The shop was rented from the owners in 1851 by Cadmus, who apparently needed more kilns to feed his growing business; he in turn gave way in 1852 to James Carr, who in association with Thomas Locker and Joseph Wooten ran it until 1855, rebuilding the works once after a fire in August 1854.

One might reasonably assume that little production could result from such an uncertain chain of management. In fact, a wide variety of yellowware is attributed to the Swan Hill Pottery. Cadmus made heavily embossed pitchers, cow creamers, inkwells, and foot warmers; while a Carr price list from 1852–55 indicates manufacture of no less than fourteen different categories, including such unusual items as saltcellars and mustard pots.

From Carr, this kiln passed once again to Joseph Wooten, who ran it from 1856 to 1858, when it was transferred to Charles Coxon. When Coxon was replaced in 1860 by John L. Rue, the factory entered upon a period of stability. J. L. Rue & Company remained active at South Amboy until 1871.

A comparison of the Carr price list with one put out in the 1860s by the Rue firm indicates the direction in which the yellowware market was moving. Originally seen as an exotic ceramic, fit for dining room and parlor, by the sixties yellowware was being relegated to utility status and the obscurity of the kitchen and pantry. Where Henderson had made elaborate pitchers and even Carr could sell salts, mustards, "Grape ice pitchers," and dinner plates, Rue offered nothing but chamberpots, pie plates, and mixing bowls. The glory days were over!

However, the area of New Jersey west of Staten Island remained an important center of yellowware production throughout much of the nineteenth century. At Perth Amboy across the Raritan River from South Amboy, Alfred Hall & Sons employed the master craftsman Enoch Wood, who had worked at Bennington's United States Pottery. From 1866 until 1880, this firm made a variety of yellow-glazed wares, including teapots, baking dishes, and bathroom items. In 1876 it was awarded a medal at the Philadelphia Centennial Exhibition.

Also located in Perth Amboy was W. H. Benton's Eagle Pottery, which manufactured yellowware snuff jars, pitchers, creamers, and bowls during the period 1858–65.

Woodbridge, two miles north of Perth Amboy, was the home of the Salamander Works, which was established in 1825 and burned down in 1896. During the period 1836–50 this firm was owned by two Frenchmen, Michael Lefoulon and Henry DeCasse, who manufactured a wide range of yellowware including Toby mugs and hound-handled pitchers.

And just three miles farther up the pike was Rahway, site of a small and apparently unsuccessful pottery operated circa 1868–70 by one William Turner. Little is known of Turner or his products.

Union and Elizabeth, both a few miles north of Rahway, had much larger factories. Haidle & Zipfh, located in the former community from 1875 until the turn of the century, was primarily a stoneware manufacturer, but the firm did produce a limited amount of utilitarian yellowware in its shop at the corner of First and Third streets.

In Elizabeth was the factory of John M. Pruden, whose father Keene had made stoneware since 1820. When he took over the shop in 1835, John expanded the inventory to include yellowware. This was made until the kiln was sold in 1879 to L. B. Beerbower & Company. It

appears that the latter concentrated thereafter on ironstone china. The firm was shut down in 1897.

The adjacent city of Newark had only a single yellowware factory, that of Balthaser Krumreich. Founded by the German potter in 1836, this small shop remained in the family until 1900. Its output consisted primarily of utilitarian items.

In western New Jersey the great pottery center was Trenton. However, major kilns were not built there until after 1850, and most potters directed their interests to white earthenwares, which were increasing in popularity at the time. One of the first firms to establish itself in Trenton was the International Pottery, whose principals were James Taylor, an East Liverpool potter, and Henry Speeler. This shop made yellowware from 1852 until 1856. Thereafter, Speeler established his own firm, the Speeler Pottery Company, which operated until it was purchased in 1879 by James Carr and Edward Clark, who used it to make white earthenware. During the Speeler era this factory produced both yellowware and Rockingham, examples of which were exhibited at the United States Potters' Association display as part of the Philadelphia Centennial in 1876.

A second major yellowware factory was built in 1852 by William H. Young, Richard Millington, and John Astbury. Known as the Carrol Street Pottery, this firm was active until 1857, when Young withdrew to form his own company, which came to be known as the Excelsior Pottery. Located on Southward Street in Trenton, Young's shop made yellowware, including a rare book flask. However, by the time that it won a bronze medal at the Philadelphia Centennial, the company, now known as William Young's Sons, was producing whitewares. This was the usual course with Trenton potteries which, if they made it at all, produced yellowware only for a few years before moving into the whiteware field. According to the *Scientific American* of August 16, 1879, by that date Trenton had sixteen potteries employing 3,000 men—yet only one was still making yellowware.

Following Young's departure, Millington and Astbury continued alone until 1859, when they took in a third partner, a man by the name of Poulson. Within a year they had ceased to make yellowware, continuing to 1870 as manufacturers of ironstone china.

Another of the few known Trenton yellowware makers was Ira W. Corey & Company. Corey with his partner Lawton opened a shop on Mill Street in 1867, and the so-called Mill Street Pottery advertised household yellowware until 1870.

New York

Despite its early start with the Tivoli Works, and despite the fact that it was a major producer of stoneware, porcelain, redware, and white earthenwares, New York was never an important yellowware center. The frequent appearance of "Rockingham" vessels on the price lists issued by New York stoneware makers might lead one to think that yellow clay was in frequent use about the state. However, careful examination shows this not to have been the case. The so-called Rockingham pitchers, flowerpots, and spittoons invariably turn out on examination to be made of stoneware clay coated with brown Albany slip. A rare exception is a finely molded and beautifully glazed spittoon made and marked by Otto V. Lewis of Mechanicville, circa 1860. This is definitely composed of yellow clay, but it is not known whether Lewis made other yellowware.

Yellowware was made to some extent in one community—Syracuse in the north-central portion of the state. In the 1860s, William H. Farrar of that city advertised himself as a maker of yellowware; and Charles W. Coykendall & Company who succeeded Farrar at his Furnace Street Pottery manufactured "corn colored ware," yet another euphemism for a familiar product. However, Coykendall was in business for only three years, being bought out in 1871 by the Onondaga Pottery Company, which commenced the manufacture of ironstone.

Another short-lived Syracuse yellowware maker was the firm of Charles W. Manchester and Fisher W. Clark, which made Rockingham and yellowware on Exchange Street during 1868–69. A successor, Thomas G. White, active only in 1870, also listed himself in the local business directory as a maker of these wares.

Finally, it should be noted that some have been misled by an 1896 price list issued by the Syracuse Stoneware Company, which claimed to be "manufacturers of Rockingham and yellowware." Indeed it was, but the pie plates, nappies, bowls, chambers, mugs, and bedpans illustrated were not made in Syracuse. Only an office and warehouse were located there, while the factory itself was in East Liverpool, Ohio. Another upstate works, the Central New York Pottery (better known as White's), advertised itself in 1890 as "Manufacturers of . . . Rockingham, Yellow and C. C. Wares," but no yellowware traceable to this firm is presently known.

At present the only other New York State company known to have employed yellow clay is the New York City Pottery, established in 1856 on West 13th Street. The founder, James Carr, had worked at South Amboy prior to coming to Manhattan, and he was thoroughly familiar with the properties of the yellow clay. There is no doubt that he used it, at least briefly, in New York, because there is in a private collection an elaborately molded Rockingham pitcher of yellow clay bearing the firm's mark. However, Carr and his partners turned swiftly to the manufacture, first of majolica, and later of ironstone, so he probably made little yellowware.

Vermont

A much more important center was located at Bennington, Vermont, where yellowware was made from about 1844 until 1858. The ware was introduced sometime in 1844 by Christopher Webber Fenton, who was then a partner of his brother-in-law Julius Norton, owner of the highly successful local stoneware kiln. The variety of wares made is unknown, but there are a few pitchers bearing the Norton/Fenton mark.

When this partnership broke up in December 1847, Fenton went into business on his own. His first advertisement, published in the *Vermont Gazette* for December 1, 1847, advised the public that he was the "Manufacturer of Yellow Fire Proof Ware." From this time on, in various partnerships primarily under the name United States Pottery Company, Fenton manufactured yellowware as one of the standard lines in a business that focused chiefly on porcelain and Rockingham.

Though marked examples are uncommon, a wide variety of yellowware has been attributed to Bennington. Included are not only common wares such as milk pans, custard cups, bakers, pie plates, and pitchers but also such novelties as embossed pipkins, Toby snuff jars, mantel decorations in the form of poodle dogs, and cow creamers.

A few such pieces have been found to bear the Bennington 1849 mark and others have been identified by form. For example, yellowware cow creamers made at Bennington are distinguished from similar products of other factories by the fact that they have open, clearly defined eyes, crescent-form nostrils, and ribs and neck folds that can be both seen and easily felt.

Price lists, local histories, and other material have associated several other Vermont communities including Burlington, St. Alban's, and Fairfax with the manufacture of Rockingham; and it has been assumed that the pitchers, flowerpots, teapots, and spittoons made by these firms were of a yellow clay body. However, examination has so far proven that attributed examples were of a buff or gray stoneware, a body similar to that used in the Rockingham made in upstate New York kilns.

Pennsylvania

Pennsylvania possessed rich supplies of yellow clay, and the state had far more important manufacturers than it has been credited with. In fact, the mark of one of these firms, J. E. Jeffords of Philadelphia, is probably the most common of all nineteenth-century yellowware cyphers. Jeffords, who had been trained by James Carr of South Amboy and Manhattan, established his Philadelphia City Pottery in 1868, and the shop remained in the family until 1904. The foreman and designer for some years was Stephen Theiss, a Belgian who had worked at Bennington from 1850 to 1858 and later at South Amboy and Worcester, Massachusetts. Theiss is said to have been one of the finest all-around potters to work at Bennington, and his skills are reflected in the wide range of yellowware produced at the Philadelphia City Pottery.

Marked examples bear either an impressed or a later stamped logo, and include teapots, pipkins, pie plates, and oval bakers. In 1876 the firm won a medal for these wares at the Philadelphia Centennial.

There were several other important Philadelphia manufactories. The shop of Captain John Mullowny has already been mentioned. James and Thomas Haig took over the pottery which their father had established on Fourth Street in 1812 and began to manufacture yellowware around 1833, continuing with this product until 1890. Among the wares attributed to this shop are cow creamers, banks in the form of log cabins, and pitchers shaped like human heads.

Another son of a prominent father was Abraham Miller, whose father, Andrew, had begun to make redware in Philadelphia in 1785. The younger Miller's pottery, known as the Spring Garden Pottery, was originally on James Street, though a second shop was established in 1851 on nearby Callowhill Street.

By 1857, Miller's advertisement in the Philadelphia Business Directory listed "white, yellow and Rockingham ware . . . made promptly to order in any quantity. . . ." The firm ceased operations around 1860, and attributed examples are rare.

Another long-time Philadelphia concern was the Market Street Pottery, established in 1810 as a stoneware works. By the 1860s it was in the hands of Galloway & Graff, whose notice in the *Crockery and Glass Journal* of 1874 advised the public that they made "Yellow and Stoneware." This shop is thought to have been active from 1868 to around 1900.

Chester County, directly west of Philadelphia, had several shops which produced yellowware. The Phoenix Pottery at Phoenixville was opened in 1867 by W. A. H. Schreiber. It had three kilns and in the 1870 census is listed as employing twenty workers and having turned out yellowware and Rockingham in the value of $14,223. Despite its success, this kiln was sold in 1879 to Henry Griffen, David Smith, and William Hill, who discontinued the manufacture of yellowware in 1882 in order to concentrate on the majolica for which the company became well known.

At nearby Oxford was a much shorter-lived factory. In 1869, Fulton C. and Samuel D. Hutchinson began to manufacture yellowware, stoneware, and redware. Their modest concern was listed in the 1870 census as employing only six men and producing but $5,500 in ware. Small wonder that they assigned for the benefit of creditors in 1872. A local bank acquired the shop and sold it in '74 to one Samuel H. Beech. Although the *Oxford Daily News* of August 5, 1874, proudly announced that "S. H. Beech has built a new kiln at his pottery in Oxford Borough and will burn a kiln of Rockingham and yellowware next week," Beech too was unfortunate. By the middle of 1875 the bank had repossessed the works.

Other Chester County yellowware makers were Edwin Brosius of Kennet Square, who is thought to have made the ware around 1870–80 (he is listed in Witmer's 1873 *Atlas of Chester County* as a "manufacturer of . . . Yellow Ware"), and William Schofield, a redware potter on Chestnut Street in Honey Brook who used plaster of Paris molds to turn out a limited amount of such ware in the 1890s.

Some of the earliest Pennsylvania yellowware makers worked in the Pittsburgh area, where in 1827 Jabez Vodrey and a partner by the name of Frost built a kiln at East Liberties (now part of greater Pittsburgh). The proprietors had brought in several Staffordshire potters and hoped to make white earthenware; but, finding the local clay unsuitable, they manufactured yellowware for three years before moving downriver to Louisville, Kentucky.

Another more successful attempt was made in 1844 when the Bennett brothers, Daniel, Edwin, and William, who had been working with James Bennett at East Liverpool, decided to establish a kiln in Pittsburgh. Called the Pennsylvania Pottery, and located in the southern end of the city, this shop turned out a substantial quantity of yellow and Rockingham ware. An elaborate paneled pitcher with mask-form spout was exhibited by the firm at the 1846 Franklin Institute in Philadelphia.

One after another the Bennett brothers left Pittsburgh until there was only Daniel. He remained active in the city until at least 1860, and frequent references in local business directories indicate that his was a substantial manufactory.

Maryland

In 1846, Edwin Bennett moved from Pittsburgh to Baltimore, where he established a small kiln for the making of yellow and Rockingham wares. He was joined by his brother William two years later, and they remained in association until 1856. Thereafter, Edwin was sole owner of the factory, which by 1880 had five separate kilns and employed a hundred workers.

Bennett produced a great number of different yellowware forms, including bowls, bakers, pie plates, molds, and elaborate pitchers and mugs. Many of these pieces were designed by Charles Coxon, who left the firm in 1863 to found Coxon & Company in Trenton, New Jersey.

Edwin Bennett was also something of an innovator. In 1858 he patented an airtight preserve jar, and yellowware examples of this form bearing his name and patent date can be found.

By 1870 the Bennett factory had begun to focus on whitewares, which it continued to make until 1936. Bennett's only real competition in the yellowware field came from the Chesapeake Pottery, which was established in 1879 by three English potters: John Tunstall, and Henry and Isaac Brougham. Never a large manufactory, it had only two buildings and a single kiln. This concern was sold in 1882 to D. F. Haynes, who converted it to the production of white earthenwares. Authenticated Chesapeake Pottery yellowware is understandably rare.

Ohio

There is little doubt that the state of Ohio constitutes the major source of American yellow-ware, and that within the state, East Liverpool was the most important center. This community on the Ohio River at the eastern border of the state was during the second half of the nineteenth century the site of dozens of different potteries, most of which at one time or another made yellowware and the related Rockingham.

The earliest proprietor was James Bennett, a Derbyshire craftsman, who arrived in this country in 1834. Bennett worked first for David Henderson at Jersey City, then walked all the way west to Troy, Indiana, where he was briefly employed at the shop of James Clews. Following this and a brief stint in Cincinnati, Bennett arrived in East Liverpool in late 1839. There, funded by local businessmen, he opened a small, single kiln works at the corner of Jefferson and Second streets in the spring of 1840.

The beginnings were modest enough: the first kilnful—"mugs, jugs, pans and other domestic wares"—netted $250. Times were hard and business slow. By 1846, James and his brothers, who had joined him on the Ohio, had left for Pittsburgh, and the shop was in the hands of another owner, Thomas Croxall. It was destroyed by flood in 1852.

However, the groundwork had been laid; soon other potters rushed to take advantage of the unique combination of rich clay beds, river transportation, and booming markets which the East Liverpool area offered. Benjamin Harker, who owned clay beds in the valley, built the second kiln late in 1840; this was to become known as the Etruria Pottery and to remain active into the 1930s.

In 1842, the Mansion House Pottery of Salt and Mear was established on Washington Street, and two years later John Goodwin, who had worked for Harker, opened his own works on Market Street. Yet another kiln was that of Ball & Morris, the Union Pottery, at Cherry Alley and Southeast Second. This was built in 1845. Then in 1847 William Brunt began work at Market Street, Woodward & Vodrey in the Herculaneum Pottery on East Fourth, and John Henderson at the corner of Broadway and St. Clair.

One should not assume that all this activity indicated unalloyed progress and booming success. The early manufacturers encountered great difficulties. With a number of yellow-ware makers flooding the local market, ware often had to be sold at a loss to be sold at all, and it was customary not only to accept produce such as chickens, eggs, and wheat in exchange but also to pay workers in the same manner. During a severe recession in 1854 one factory was able to pay only a dollar a month in cash; the rest was in orders redeemable at local stores with which the factory owner had arranged credit. Turmoil and uncertainty of this sort led inevitably to failures, and during the 1840s and 1850s more East Liverpool concerns went bankrupt than remained in business. Nevertheless, potters continued to flock to the area: by 1853 there were eleven different potteries with nearly four hundred employees and a total annual output of $175,000. Almost all of this was yellowware.

Since little of this early ware was marked or can otherwise be identified, we must turn to the few remaining price lists and catalogues to determine what was being made in East Liverpool. One thing is clear. The local potters were practical men. They had little illusion about selling the more decorative wares that were made in New Jersey and Vermont. Utility was what their customers wanted. An 1850 price list issued by John Goodwin indicated clearly what sold in Ohio. Chamberpots headed the list, followed by pitchers, bowls, milk pans, butter tubs, mugs, nappies, dishes, pie plates, and flowerpots.

While other items came and went over the years, most of these pieces remained staples at East Liverpool throughout the second half of the nineteenth century. Thus, an 1864 price list for the Vodrey Pottery Works included nappies, milk pans, jelly cans (preserve jars), bowls, bedpans, baking dishes, pie plates, chambers, mugs, pitchers, and butter pots; while as late as 1892 the catalogue of the D. E. McNichol Pottery Company illustrated bowls, milk pans, butter jars, pitchers, baking dishes, nappies, pie plates, and chamberpots.

This is not to imply, however, that the ware was of inferior quality. Most of it was sturdy and some was quite attractive. East Liverpool potteries sold throughout the United States, and some of their products gained national recognition. In 1876, Samuel and William Baggott, who had purchased John Goodwin's shop in 1853, exhibited their yellow and Rockingham wares at the Philadelphia Centennial, where they had a prominent place in the booth of the United States Potters' Association.

An exhaustive listing of the many East Liverpool potteries will be found in the Appendix; there would be little purpose in recounting their histories here, particularly as in most cases little more than beginning and ending dates, products, and names of partners is known. However, in some cases tales have come down to us that throw an interesting light on the men behind the business. For example, money was usually tight at the kilns, and the owners desperate to obtain further funds. In one instance, William Brunt, Jr., and his brother-in-law William Bloor, who were operating a kiln established in 1847 by Brunt's father, decided to join the California gold rush in an effort to find some quick cash. Unlike most, they were lucky, returning in 1855 with some $10,000 in gold dust. This infusion of capital saved the business, which continued to operate until the 1930s.

Another discovery marked the end of a yellowware manufactory. Following the death in 1875 of their father, the pioneer yellowware maker John Goodwin and his sons James and

George sought to convert the works to whitewares. However, they lacked the necessary funds and would have been forced to remain in their current business had not a third son, James, brought his offspring to play in his grandfather's house. In the course of a bit of rough and tumble, the boy knocked over an old rocker. Out rolled $5,000 in bonds which John Goodwin had secreted there! The sons cashed them and made their conversion.

There were also yellowware potteries at Wellsville, a few miles southwest of East Liverpool, and at Newell, West Virginia, just across the Ohio River. The largest concern was John Patterson & Sons, established in 1882 and active under various managements well into this century. The Pattersons turned out many different items, including tobacco humidors, teapots, cups, mugs, dishes, bowls, and nappies. A much earlier but unsuccessful establishment, that of George and John Garner in partnership with Enoch Bullock, had operated from 1845 to 1847. Newell had but a single yellowware manufactory, the Virginia Pottery, which was located on Grant Street. It opened and closed in one year—1848.

The other major Ohio yellowware manufacturing center was Cincinnati, also located on the Ohio River but in the far southwestern corner of the state. Though much remains to be learned of their work, it is evident that the Cincinnati potters played an important role in developing the Ohio industry.

The first to make yellowware here appear to have been James Doane (c. 1831–37) and Uriah Kendall & Sons. The latter firm converted from redware to yellowware around 1840, and remained active under various names until 1870. The impressed mark, U. KENDALL & SONS/ CINCINNATI, is one of the few to identify ware from the city.

Other early concerns included that founded in 1849 by William Bromley, whose Brighton Pottery remained in business until around 1860, and the Dayton Street Pottery owned from 1859 by Samuel Pollock and family. This firm was sold around 1874 to Patrick L. Coultry and James Maloney, who advertised their "Rockingham and Yellowware . . . and Air Tight Fruit Jars" in the 1874–75 edition of the *Crockery and Glass Journal*.

Apparently business was as difficult here as in East Liverpool, for the many different firms listed in the Appendix reflect frequent failures and changes of management. However, there were also stable and successful manufactories, such as those of Peter Lessel and his descendants, active from 1848 until 1900, and the family of George Peter Behn, which maintained its business from 1857 until the turn of the century.

Advertisements and existing examples indicate that the Cincinnati potteries were even more conservative than those at East Liverpool. Evidently nothing other than the most basic wares, pie plates, bowls, bakers, and the ubiquitous chamberpots were made here.

Another important center was Zanesville on the Muskingum River in east-central Ohio. The two major establishments were Bernard Howson & Company and the Pyatt pottery.

Howson, with partners John Hallam and George Wheaton, began to make yellowware here in 1840. After several management changes his son John assumed control, remaining active until the business was sold for other use in 1874. Unlike many of his contemporaries, John Howson was an innovative potter. Besides the usual pie plates and bowls, he made such odd and interesting things as Staffordshire-type dogs (which served as mantelpiece ornaments and door stops), book flasks, toothbrush holders, and even asthma inhalers.

The Pyatt firm was established in 1849 by George Pyatt, who worked in Zanesville until he removed to Missouri in 1859. Returning in 1866, he reestablished his business, which passed in 1879 to a son, J. G. Pyatt. Known as the Tremont Pottery, this shop existed until 1900.

Two other long-lived establishments were the Star Pottery, owned by Calvin Bumbaugh, in business from 1873 to 1900, and the pottery of Jacob S. King and John T. Swope, which remained active from 1879 until after the turn of the century.

A few miles south of Zanesville is the town of Roseville, Ohio, and here was located one of the most important twentieth-century yellowware producers. The Robinson, Ransbottom Pottery began making utilitarian yellowware in the 1930s, and most of its pre-1950 wares are considered collectible. The impressed mark R.R.P. CO. is familiar to most collectors. The firm remains in production. Another manufacturer of the same period is the A. E. Hull Pottery Company of Crooksville, a neighboring community. Established in 1905, Hull introduced art pottery in 1917, and thereafter was best known for this product. However, its blue-banded "Golden Yellow Ware" (to quote a 1914 ad in the trade publication *China, Glass and Lamps*) was an important staple for over a decade.

There were potteries in other areas as well. Akron, in northeastern Ohio, had at least two yellowware manufacturers: Rowley & Baker, active circa 1850–57, and Johnson, Whitman & Company, which was in business from 1857 until about 1864. Another Baker, Herbert, was in business at Middlebury, Ohio, with Enoch Raleigh from 1850 until 1852. By and large, though, such outlying kilns never were able successfully to compete with the great factories of East Liverpool, Cincinnati, and Zanesville.

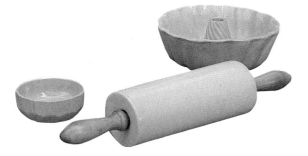

Yellowware Potteries in Other States

Yellow clays were widely dispersed throughout the Middle West, and potteries were established in several states. In New England, on the other hand, the few firms that attempted this ware relied on imported soil, an added cost factor that usually assured their early demise.

THE MIDWEST

One of the oldest yellowware manufactories in the Midwest grew out of a pottery erected in 1837 at Troy, Indiana, a tiny town on the Ohio River east of Evansville. James Clews, who had been a successful whiteware manufacturer in England, brought forty potters here in the hopes of establishing an "American Staffordshire." The clay proved ill-suited for his purposes, and many of his workmen succumbed to illness. Within a year Clews was gone, and the pottery was occupied in 1839 by Jabez Vodrey, who made passable yellowware until 1846 when he began a promising career in East Liverpool. The Troy kiln, which had to be rebuilt following a fire, was then run from 1851 to 1863 by James Saunders and Samuel Wilson, and from 1865 to 1888 by Benjamin Hincho. Much yellowware made here has been found in the vicinity, and the shop was one of the state's most important.

The most interesting, though certainly not the most successful of yellowware works in Illinois was located at Peoria, where, following the collapse of his Bennington enterprise, Christopher Webber Fenton convinced a group of local businessmen to invest in a gigantic "departmental pottery" to employ over a thousand workers and to produce in its several branches stoneware, yellowware, Rockingham, and various forms of brick.

For sheer audacity, this project exceeded anything undertaken in the nineteenth-century American pottery world. Even the local Bennington, Vermont, newspaper, still smarting from the loss of the town's most important industry, admitted that "we can but admire his [Fenton's] praiseworthy efforts to rid this country of her abject dependence on Great Britain for an article so indispensable to the comfort and convenience of the people at large." Reality of the venture was something else. Though a portion of the great manufactory was erected in 1859, it was not until the following year that the first ware was fired. The Rockingham and yellowware produced, often with the use of molds which had been employed at Bennington, was adequate enough; but costs were too high and the anticipated market never developed. The firm collapsed in 1863, and Fenton died in an accident two years later.

The works were reactivated in 1864 by A. M. Johnson as the American Pottery Company, remaining in business until 1873 and turning out a substantial number of simple yellowware forms.

Another local concern was the Morton Pottery Company, located at the community of the same name a few miles southeast of Peoria. From 1910 until the 1930s, this firm turned out a wide variety of yellowware articles. A 1920s catalogue illustrates mixing bowls, nappies, custards, and the so-called Old English Stein Set, a grouping of pitcher and six matching mugs, all banded in blue. Not too hard to find today, these wares most often bear on their bases the impressed mark of the company by whom they were offered as a premium: 100% PURE/BUCKEYE.

The promise of rich clay banks at Kaolin, Missouri, encouraged George Pyatt of Zanesville to settle there in 1859 as manager of a pottery owned by Elihu Shepard. Though he was able to produce adequate yellowware, he could not make a profit; and he returned to Zanesville in '64, reestablishing his own business two years later. The Kaolin firm reverted to Shepard, who had been active there in partnership with Frederick Woolford since 1852. They made yellowware until about 1865.

In terms of sheer quantity of ware available to collectors, one of the most important of all Midwestern potteries is the Red Wing Union Stoneware Company of Red Wing, Minnesota, even though this firm did not begin to make yellowware until the 1920s. Red Wing, the amalgamation of several earlier stoneware works, introduced its Spongeband line around 1929. This ware had a yellow body and a narrow band of red sponging between two blue lines. Pitchers, casseroles, refrigerator jars, cake stands, reamers, and batter bowls were among the items produced. A few years later similar forms were manufactured in the so-called Saffron Ware line, which was characterized by a yellow body embellished by a single white between two brown slip lines. Many of these pieces bore the imprint: RED WING/SAFFRON/WARE.

Saffron Ware was made by Red Wing until 1967, and vast quantities of yellowware from this source are available. While a few people may feel that such ware is of too recent vintage, the majority of collectors embrace it for its abundance and variety.

THE BORDER STATES AND THE SOUTH

Only a few yellowware potteries existed south of Pennsylvania and Ohio. Among them, those of Maryland were certainly most important. However, there were other kilns. In Delaware, the only known manufactory was that of Abner Marshall, who worked in Hockessin, a small community just west of Wilmington. Though he was active from 1859 to 1866 and turned out both Rockingham and yellowware, little else is known of his wares.

Farther south, at Kaolin, South Carolina, some six miles from Augusta, Georgia, William H. Farrar, one of the major Bennington stockholders, established a pottery in 1856. Although its main purpose was to produce whitewares and even porcelain, this kiln had by 1858 begun to turn out excellent yellowware. Reorganized circa 1859–60 as the Southern Porcelain Company, the works operated until destroyed by fire in 1864.

There was a much earlier pottery at Louisville, Kentucky, where in 1829 William Lewis established a yellowware works. He was moderately successful, employing Jabez Vodrey as a turner and general supervisor until 1839. In that year, however, Vodrey departed for the ill-fated Troy, Indiana, enterprise; lacking its guiding star, the Louisville Pottery closed soon after. It was almost a century later that another yellowware manufacturer located here. This was the Louisville Pottery Company, which operated in the 1920s.

NEW ENGLAND

With the exception of Bennington, little yellowware was made in this area of the country. Various stoneware manufactories advertised as the "Importers and manufacturers of stone-ware, yellowware, etc." but in almost all cases the stoneware was manufactured: the yellow-ware was imported. Attempts were made, though. As far back as 1832, Noah S. and George Day of Norwalk, Connecticut, were advertising for "Three or four apprentices to the Earthen and Yellow Ware business. . . ." There is no known yellowware associated with this firm, although it was for decades renowned for its stoneware and redware.

An 1880 catalogue of the Lamson Pottery at Exeter, New Hampshire, illustrates what are clearly yellowware pie plates and four sizes of white-banded mugs, yet factory records do not indicate that such wares were ever produced there. A similar situation exists as regards the A. E. Smith & Sons Pottery of Norwalk, Connecticut, and the Somerset Potters Works of Somerset, Massachusetts, both of whom have been cited as yellowware manufacturers.

In fact, only one New England concern can be assuredly credited with the production of yellowware. This is the Boston Earthenware Manufactory, established in 1854 by Frederick H. Mear, who had previously run the Mansion House Pottery in East Liverpool. One of the major investors in the firm was William F. Homer, who owned the premises and periodically appears as a proprietor. Though the works remained on Condor Street in East Boston, the name of this factory changed over the years, first to the East Boston Crockery Manufactory, then, after its purchase in 1876 by Thomas Gray and Lyman W. Clark, to the New England Pottery Company. By 1878 ironstone was being made here, and from then until the factory closed in 1914 white earthenwares were its main output. There is no doubt, though, that yellowware was made during the early years. Advertisements allude specifically to the "manufacture" of yellow and Rockingham wares, and examples bearing the impressed mark BOSTON EARTHENWARE MAN-UFACTURING CO. are known.

On the other hand, recent citations of the Bangor, Maine, Stoneware Company as a yellowware manufacturer are definitely in error. This firm produced quantities of stoneware, but its advertisements clearly distinguish between this and the yellowware and Rockingham for which it served as a wholesale and retail distributor of other firms' wares.

CALIFORNIA

California was an early prolific source of yellowware, and examples bearing the marks of later kilns are often seen on the West Coast. The first known manufactory was Daniel Brannon's Pioneer Pottery, located on Twelfth Avenue in East Oakland. It was established in 1856 and by the 1880s could boast of three kilns and a substantial output.

The Pacific Clay Manufacturing Company was established at Elsinore by 1884, later moving to South Riverside, a suburb of Los Angeles. This firm remained active until 1910; its bowls and custard cups marked PACIFIC are fairly common. The J. A. Bauer & Company pottery in Los Angeles lasted even longer, from 1890 to 1958. Its line consisted in the 1920s of "yellow bowls, crocks, vases and ollas," the latter a traditional southwestern product.

British and Canadian Yellowware Makers

The making of yellowware commenced in the British Isles in the late eighteenth century and continued well into the 1900s. Likewise, there were several active Canadian manufacturers during the second half of the nineteenth century. These wares were imported into the United States both at the time they were being made, and, in more recent years, by dealers and collectors. Consequently, the American collector will frequently encounter non-American pieces. Foreign makers of the more commonly seen wares are discussed in the Appendix.

Many collectors look for yellowware, period. Its origin is unimportant to them. However, many others would seek, ideally, to own only American-made examples. Short of acquiring only marked pieces, that is seldom possible, for examination of period catalogues and price sheets makes it clear that many essentially identical forms were made on both sides of the Atlantic. As an example, a 1926 catalogue issued by Church Gresley of Derbyshire, England, illustrated nappies, lipped or batter bowls, colanders (called culenders in England), and custard cups (pudding bowls), which were in every way identical to similar items made in this country. Given this situation, it is unrealistic at best to hope to distinguish among many of the more common forms.

Some generalizations may be made, though: English wares are more varied and in many cases more delicately potted. Catalogues and marked pieces include forms such as honey jars, covered bowls, round and oval casseroles, brawn pots, lipped nappies, lipped milk pans, and rice jars which do not appear to have been made in this country. Also, in many (but by no means all) cases English wares are thinner-walled, have more elaborate handles, are more sharply and carefully embossed, and have a more classic look than their American counterparts. For example, compare the two mugs, one English, one American, in illustration 37 (page 71). However, all such generalities are subject to exception. Certainly the fine early New Jersey wares rival anything in this medium ever manufactured in the British Isles. Moreover, the Canadian wares, often made by expatriate American potters, are in most instances largely indistinguishable from those made south of the border.

It should also be noted that while English potters produced much more Mocha decorated ware and for a much longer period (Church Gresley was still advertising salts, mustards, and peppers in the 1920s), it was made in the United States as well. Edwin Bennett manufactured Mocha mugs at Baltimore, and a C. C. Thompson & Company, East Liverpool, Ohio, catalogue of 1886 illustrates Mocha-decorated mixing bowls and chamberpots. Likewise, though it was more common for English firms to glaze the interiors of their yellowware vessels in white, this cannot serve to distinguish the imported wares since various American firms alluded to their "white lined" yellowware.

One category of foreign yellowware can be clearly distinguished. Collectors will frequently encounter finely potted, sometimes in part hand-built, pieces which bear no resemblance to other American, English, or Canadian wares. These are usually highly decorative matchboxes, condiment holders, or table centerpieces, often embellished with fish and animal forms and in some cases bearing traces of gilding. Some examples are impressed A. TSCHINKEL or simply A.T. These are unquestionably of Continental origin.

Faced with such problems of attribution, what should the collector do? For those who collect only the ware, without regard to origin, there is no worry. On the other hand, those who would try to limit their field to American-made examples but who do not wish to suffer the severe limitation of focusing only on marked pieces are best advised to collect examples which most closely resemble those that bear American marks or appear in the advertising materials produced by American potteries.

Yellowware Forms

To the casual observer and beginning collector, yellowware may seem a rather limited field: a few crocks, more jars and pie plates, and lots and lots of bowls. Yet the number of forms made in this medium is greater than that to be found in any other field of American ceramics. Only redware can rival it for variety. It is true, however, that many of these vessels are quite uncommon.

Bowls

By far the most common yellowware form was the bowl. Nearly every factory produced them from the 1830s until World War II. Wheel-turned or "plain" bowls, as they were termed, were made in as many as a dozen nested sizes from 3″ to 17″ in diameter. Some were un-decorated, others bore slip banding in various color combinations with brown and white predominating. For collectors seeking a complete nest or set, the most readily obtainable are bowls bearing a single wide white band (advertised in ten sizes by the Morton, Illinois, Pottery Company, c. 1920–30), three thin white bands, or two white within two brown bands.

Less common but still readily obtainable are molded bowls. These may bear an overall embossed decorative design (often floral) or may combine this with slip decoration. Often referred to in advertising as "pressed" bowls, these also were found in up to ten nesting sizes from less than 5″ to 14″.

Harder to find are twelve-sided, molded bowls, and examples either turned or molded which have Mocha decoration. Once believed to have been made only in England, these were pictured in late nineteenth-century sales catalogues issued by various American firms, including C. C. Thompson & Company of East Liverpool, Ohio. Since like most bowls, these were rarely marked, it is usually not possible to distinguish American examples from those produced in the British Isles. Another rarity is the outsized bowl. Though standard sizes did not exceed 18″, larger ones were made, probably for institutional use. The Clinton, New Jersey, Historical Society owns an example fully 25″ in diameter.

Another bowl form was the "lipped" bowl, which incorporated a spout in the rim and was designed for the mixing of cake or pancake batter, hence the contemporary term "batter bowl" used to refer to this type. Lipped bowls were produced in fewer sizes, usually from 8″ to 12″ in diameter, but showed equal variety in decoration: embossing, banding, or Mocha work.

Colanders used for draining food were usually nothing more than bowls in the base and lower sides of which holes had been punched. These perforations might be patterned—stars, triangles, and diamonds are most common—or might simply run in circles about the bowl. Typically the colander would also have one or two holes beneath the rim through which a hanging string might be run, and semicircular cutouts in the base to allow for drainage. While the usual type was the curvilinear mixing bowl form, colanders with tapering straight sides in the manner of a nappy are found. There are also a few colanders with narrow ears or "lifts" to facilitate handling.

Nappies and Milk Pans

A vessel which often served the same purpose as the bowl—mixing, preparing, and serving food—was the nappy, a circular vessel with straight sides tapering out from the base. Found in substantial quantity even today, the nappy was made by most yellowware manufacturers. As many as thirteen nesting sizes ranging in diameter from 3″ to 13″ may be found, and nappies are among the most commonly collected of yellowware forms. They are also among the earliest, appearing in an 1850 price list of John Goodwin's Eagle Pottery at East Liverpool and a circa 1852–55 flyer from the Swan Hill kiln at South Amboy, New Jersey.

A much later type is the so-called scalloped nappy dish. This is a much more bowl-like shape, with slightly flaring sides, a pronounced rolled rim, and heavily embossed paneling. A similar example termed a "rice nappy" appears in turn of the century catalogues published by D. E. McNichol of East Liverpool, and it appears that the terms may have been used interchangeably. While the ordinary nappy might be either turned or molded, scalloped or rice nappies were always cast. They are also much less common.

Even harder to find are the "square nappies" listed in an 1891 price list for J. W. Croxall of East Liverpool, and illustrated in period catalogues. Made in seven sizes from 6″ to 12″ square, these might well be the square bakers referred to in earlier price lists.

The latest nappy form appeared in the 1920s. Referred to in manufacturers' catalogues as a "baking nappy," it was a small, twelve-sided, bowl-like vessel ranging in diameter from 4″ to 9″. Unlike its predecessors, it was decorated, bearing blue or green transfer work or delicate freehand slip designs.

Less common and easily mistaken for the older and larger nappies are milk pans. The latter may be distinguished, however, by their heavily rolled rims (nappies lack rims) and by their greater depth in relation to diameter. Milk pans were seemingly made in only four sizes, from 10″ to 14″ in diameter.

More common in stoneware and redware, the milk pan was an important kitchen and dairy accessory used in the cooling and separation of milk and cream. Before 1900 they were replaced by lighter and more durable pans in tin or graniteware.

Pitchers

Pitchers appear in catalogues from the early 1850s on, and they were made in such variety that it would be possible to build a major collection around these alone. As late as the 1870s, though, they were referred to in price lists as "jugs," a term that has led to some confusion.

Moreover, the progression in form here clearly illustrates the fallacy of claims that the earliest yellowware is the simplest. Without doubt, the style and complexity of shape found in the hound-handled, six-sided, and heavily embossed pitchers produced at potteries in Jersey City, South Amboy, and Bennington, Vermont, during the period 1830–50 was far superior to anything produced thereafter.

However, few of these pieces are available to collectors, so focus must be on the later examples. These were either wheel-turned or molded, and came in several sizes including pint, one and a half pint, quart, half gallon, and gallon. Undecorated examples are less often seen than those which were banded, touched with Mocha, or embossed. Embossing was particularly popular—everything from an early fire pumper to flowers, Gothic arches, animals, and advertising messages can be found.

Form was equally diverse. The clearest distinction is between the taller water or cider pitchers and the squat creamers or milk pitchers. However, there are so many sizes and shapes that clear boundaries are often hard to draw. Bodies may be oval (the usual case), round, or geometric. Sides may be vertical, show an inward taper from the base, have a pronounced shoulder below the neck, be ovoid, or flare outward at the rim. Spouts are sometimes quite large, at other times but a wrinkle in the rim. Embossed decoration may cover the whole piece, may determine its form as in the popular walnut-shaped pitchers, or may serve only as an adjunct to slip decoration. Bases can be elaborately molded or extremely plain. The variations are seemingly endless.

Storage Vessels

Vessels for the preservation and storage of foodstuffs are commonly found in yellow clay. Among the earliest are preserve jars, referred to in early price lists as jelly cans or fruit jars. While a major function of such vessels was the storage of jams and jellies, they were also widely used to can vegetables and even meats. Until driven from the market by the advent of the glass Mason jar, the ceramic vessels were a necessity found in every home.

Though they appeared in several shapes—octagonal, barrel-shaped, and cylindrical, with either sloping or narrow shelving shoulder—the important thing about these jars was the closure. If it could not be rendered airtight, the contents would spoil. As early as 1858, James Bennett of Baltimore patented a disklike top for his yellowware preserve jars. This was intended to be sealed with wax and covered with cloth. Other closures included an unusual screw-on clay top, tin discs sealed with wax, and gum sealers. None worked particularly well, but yellowware preserve jars continued to be made well into the 1870s.

Though extremely common in redware and stoneware, jugs which were long important in the transportation and storage of liquids such as cider, whiskey, and vinegar were seldom made in yellowware. References in early price lists to "jugs" clearly refer to pitchers; and the only yellowware jugs found today are turn-of-the-century specimens with cylindrical sides, rounded shoulders, and decoration consisting of a few slip bands.

Other early and traditional forms are equally uncommon. Ovoid cream pots, such as the one shown on the right in illustration 60 (page 87), were a basic stoneware form; but in yellowware I know only of this example. There is also an ovoid jar made by the potter Trule Stevens, at Nemaha, Nebraska, circa 1860. This unique piece is now in the collection of the Nebraska State Historical Society.

On the other hand, the cylindrical form with matching flat cover which collectors now call a crock was made in great quantity in yellow clay. These were referred to in price lists as butter jars or butter pots, and came in several sizes: pint, quart, half gallon, three quarts, gallon, and six quarts. First advertised in the 1860s, crocks continue to be made today. Some are left undecorated, while others are slip-banded, and a few bear stenciled designations such as "Butter," "Rice," or "Lard." Twentieth-century examples often bear stencil decoration and advertisers' messages.

Most American-made crocks appear to have lacked handles, but English makers' catalogues illustrate handled examples which were termed "rice jars." However, there are circa 1920–40 American examples with flattened ear handles, slightly convex sides, and embossed decoration, which are referred to as "cookie jars."

One of the earliest storage vessels was the keeler. This is a low, circular vessel with two vertical handles rising from the rim. The handles customarily are pierced so that a lifting rod may pass through them. Ceramic keelers are modeled after a much earlier wooden form which was used to cool fresh milk and for other farm chores. Examples in yellowware were referred to also as butter tubs. They lacked covers and are found both banded and undecorated. Catalogue references to this form seem confined to the 1850s, and it appears that they were not made much after that period.

Early catalogues also refer to "honey jars," though these remain unidentified. It is possible, however, that the vessels meant are the plain cone-shaped ones in illustration 24 (page 61). These originally had flat, close-fitting lids. Another form has also been traditionally known as a honey jar or honey pot, that is, the small, baluster-shaped vessel produced and marked by the Roycroft Shops of East Aurora, New York, in the early 1900s.

Other storage containers include wall-hung salt boxes with ceramic or wooden lids such as the ones made in the 1930s by the Red Wing Union Stoneware Company. Such pieces often are imprinted: RED WING/SAFFRON/WARE on the base. Red Wing produced an extensive line of yellowware during the thirties and forties under the brand name Saffron Ware. Spice sets, sometimes including a matching salt box, are also found. These may have vertically fluted bases and may be decorated with slip banding. Individual containers usually are marked to indicate their contents, as "Nutmeg," "Cloves," or "Ginger."

Baking and Cooking Utensils

In a very real sense, yellowware was intended for the kitchen and the tasks performed there. Among the earliest items cited in pottery price lists are yellowware pie plates, baking dishes, and cake pans. Some such forms were made for well over a century.

Pie plates in 7″, 8″, 9″, and 10″ diameters were listed in 1850 by the Goodwin Pottery of East Liverpool, and square pie plates from 7″ to 12″ were among the circa 1852–55 products of the Swan Hill Pottery at South Amboy, New Jersey. Round pie plates with their shallow, flaring sides are familiar to all yellowware collectors. Turned, drape-molded, or cast, some were as small as 6″, a few over 12″. Specimens marked with the names of earlier New Jersey and Pennsylvania potteries are known. There are also circa 1920–40 pieces with fluted lower sides, which were made at the Red Wing, Minnesota, pottery. Nests consisting of four to six pie plates can be assembled.

Square pie plates are also listed in early catalogues. Since no illustrations have yet been found, it is difficult to be sure exactly what these were, though it is possible that this is another instance of different names being applied to the same form. If so, square pie plates may be nothing more than the square nappies or bakers previously mentioned. At least all three described types are found in the same sizes, an interesting coincidence.

These are not the only unidentified pieces to be found in this category. Some nineteenth-century price lists also refer to "cake pans" (made in 8″, 9″, 10″, 11″, and 12″ sizes), "pound cake pans" (8.5″ and 10″), and "bakers' pans" (also in 8″, 9″, 10″, 11″, and 12″ sizes). At the moment we cannot be sure of the shapes of these vessels or whether or not the terms relate to known yellowware.

Collectors, however, are quite familiar with the rectangular and oval baking dishes or "bakers" which were advertised from the 1840s into the 1890s from New Jersey to Ohio. Referred to as "oblong bakers," the former are shallow oven dishes with sides that taper outward from the base. Made in ten sizes between 5″ and 14″ long, they form interesting if hard-to-assemble nests. Early marks found on their bases include those of Jersey City's David Henderson and Jeffords of Philadelphia.

The oval baker was also known as the "round rim" or "French style" baker, and was produced in inch sizes ranging from 6″ to 12″. The shape is much like that of contemporary oval serving dishes, and they no doubt served that function as well. Oval bakers are illustrated in a D. E. McNichol Pottery Company catalogue of the 1890s, indicating the longevity of this form. The Jeffords, Philadelphia, mark is found on some examples.

Though by no means as common as their sponge-decorated and stoneware counterparts, yellowware bean pots can be found. Earlier ones, such as those advertised in the 1870s by the Industrial Pottery Works of East Liverpool, had a single handle joined to a bulbous body. Saffron Ware examples produced during the 1930s by Minnesota's Red Wing Union Stoneware Company had two handles and a fluted lower body. Both types came with matching lids and were used in the oven to bake beans and similar dishes.

More readily available are custard cups. Also known as cake cups, and used for a variety of purposes including the making of custards and jellies, these were small items—usually ranging in height from 1.75″ to 3″. Earlier examples, such as those made in the 1850s at Bennington's United States Pottery, had sides which tapered out from the base and lacked pronounced rims. Most specimens found today date after 1890 and have a gently curving form topped by a rolled rim. Decoration varies greatly, from a plain clear glaze to embossed Gothic arches and many different combinations of slip banding.

Another cooking utensil was the pipkin, a bulbous, covered vessel with either handle or long, hollow lift that allowed steam to escape from the cooking food. The pipkin is an ancient form, and the term is applied to vessels which vary substantially in detail. Yellowware pipkins made at the United States Pottery in Bennington had a pouring spout and side handle. Pennsylvania examples had hollow handles, and those found in Canada often resemble the

Vermont form but lack its embossed decoration. Though they came in at least four different sizes, matching pipkins are rare. Marked ones are also scarce, though the Jeffords, Philadelphia, mark has been seen on a few.

Essential to the baker was the rolling pin, and examples of this utensil in yellowware are relatively common. The piece consists of a hollow ceramic cylinder into which are inserted two turned wooden handles, one of which screws into the other to form a union. Unmarked and unadvertised, these pieces have an obscure history, though they appear to have been made for a considerable period of time.

Much less common is the square or oblong meat tenderizer. These pieces have a wooden handle and were also made in stoneware. The inherent likelihood of damage when any ceramic object is used as a hammer seems to have taken its toll here. Yellowware tenderizers are among the rarest of forms.

The molds in which blancmange, a cornstarch custard pudding, or jelly was set to harden form one of the most interesting subdivisions of the yellowware field. Though similar molds may be found in white earthenware, redware, and stoneware, examples made in the yellow clay are far more common. Earliest are the so-called Turk's Head molds, with swirled interior about a central cone.

Found in much greater variety are figured molds which incorporate various plant and animal forms within a circular, tear-shaped, oval, octagonal, or free-form body. In most instances the figure that shapes the jelly or pudding is at the base of the mold, and the sides are fluted.

The most common mold forms are fruits and vegetables, including ears of corn, bunches of grapes, sheaves of wheat, asparagus, melons, and pineapples; more abstract shapes include hearts, beehives, diamonds, shells, and triangles. Most such designs are found in very small molds, many of which bear the as yet unidentified YELLOW ROCK/PHILADELPHIA stamp.

Most sought after are the figural molds incorporating humans or animals. Among the known impressions are fish, lion, boar, deer, rabbits, and at least one human figure—a fisherman. It is evident both from extant examples and from period advertisements that the most common form was the corn mold, which was made in at least three sizes, as was the sheaf of wheat variation. These have been found with makers' marks, particularly that of I. W. Cory, active in Trenton, New Jersey, circa 1867–70.

Tablewares

As previously mentioned, earlier makers of yellowware saw their product not as something utilitarian to be hidden away in kitchen, pantry, and bedroom but as a fine ceramic meant for display. Nowhere is this more evident than in the field of tablewares. Early plates, coffeepots, salts, and serving dishes manifest a desire for style and a wish to compete with the finer ceramics of the period. However, as the manufacture of white earthenwares and porcelain became established, American yellowware producers turned more and more to the ordinary.

Among the finest examples of early yellowware are the coffeepots produced in the 1830s and 1840s by D. & J. Henderson and the successor American Pottery Manufacturing Company, both of Jersey City. Classic form, elaborate embossing incorporating such traditional motifs as the goose head spout and handle in human form, mark these rare examples. Coffeepots continued to be made intermittently over the next century, the latest ones being vaguely Art Deco examples from the 1930s.

Teapots were much more common. During the mid- to late nineteenth century several Liverpool firms produced them, including John Patterson & Sons; the Globe Pottery Company, which turned out a rather extreme example with embossed strawberry vine decoration; and C. C. Thompson & Company, which made a squat form embossed in basketweave that was used as a promotional giveaway by agents for the firm manufacturing Windsor Baking Powder. Apparently the only marked examples are circa 1880–90 basketweave and floral pattern pots bearing the stamp of Jeffords of Philadelphia.

The cups in which to drink these beverages are much less common, though a few plain yellow examples with slightly ovoid bodies, ear handles, and flared rims are known. Much more frequently found are mugs, which were made for decades both here and in England. The typical shape was a turned cylinder with molded foot. Sizes included a half, full, three quarters, pint, and two pint. Variations encompassed vessels without a foot, ones with slightly concave sides, and quite a few with embossed decoration ranging from floral motifs to scenes of sportsmen afield. Most mugs were slip band–decorated, and differences in banding are so great as to make possible a sizable collection focused solely on this type. An interesting variation is the barrel-shaped mug or tankard which was embossed with staves and pins.

The earliest available price lists, dating to the 1850s, refer to plates or dishes in six sizes between 6″ and 12″, and it appears that the two terms may have been interchangeable at the time. In any case, few examples have survived. Needless to say, these shallow eating vessels, with their wide, flattened rims, should not be confused with pie plates, which were made in greater quantity and for a much longer period of time.

Far later though similar forms include deep plates or soup plates with scalloped edges and embossed Western scenes. These date to the 1900s and are probably English in origin. Presently unidentified are the "oyster dishes" ranging in size from 5″ to 9″ listed in the 1870s catalogues of the Broadway Pottery Works at Liverpool, Ohio.

Serving dishes and platters were also made in yellowware. While the oval bakers mentioned earlier doubled as serving dishes, there were numerous other pieces intended for the table. A few round vegetable dishes with crimped or fluted edges are known, and during the years 1900 to 1950 many different covered bowls and casseroles were produced. Though these varied greatly in appearance and in size (ranging in diameter from 6″ to 12″), they all showed certain general twentieth-century characteristics—heavy, banded rims, bodies that tapered in gradually from rim to foot and, in many cases, fluting or other embossed decoration. All had matching covers which in most cases rested on an interior rim, and many were slip-banded. Such pieces were produced by numerous firms, including the Red Wing Potteries (as part of their Saffron Ware and Spongeband lines), Weller, and Hull.

Much harder to come by are undecorated octagonal serving dishes similar to those commonly seen in ironstone. These pieces may bear the marks of New Jersey potteries, and most date prior to 1850.

Related octagonal platters were another early form. A rare example in the collection of the East Liverpool Museum of Ceramics bears the mark: BENNETT & BROTHERS, 1842. Similar platters with New Jersey and Philadelphia marks are known.

Later but almost equally scarce are platters with scalloped edges and embossed cross-hatching as decoration. Though presently unidentified, it is thought that these pieces are Midwestern and date from the late nineteenth century.

Trivets which were placed under hot dishes are extremely rare. A few examples exhibiting a grillwork within a circular form are known. Like most specialty items, trivets were not listed in pottery advertising.

Condiments and seasonings were even more important in the nineteenth century than they are today since meats, particularly, were not always in the best state of preservation, and salts, peppers, and mustard pots were among the first American yellowware. James Carr's Swan Hill Pottery at South Amboy was offering salts at twenty-five cents per dozen and mustards at fifty cents for the same number during the period 1852–55. Yet by the 1860s, his successor, John L. Rue, had dropped both forms from inventory. In fact, it would appear that few American firms made these vessels after 1860. On the other hand English manufacturers produced them well into the twentieth century, and most examples found here can be traced to that source.

Salts, which may be either individual or master depending upon size, were traditionally made in the form of a bowl mounted on a turned foot or pedestal. The type is of great antiquity. In the Middle Ages, when salt was often hard to come by, it was deemed an honor to sit near the master salt, which was placed to the right of the head of household. Hence the term "below the salt."

Most yellowware salts seen today are decorated with slip banding, sometimes combined with Mocha work. Seaweed and earthworm are the typical patterns. One will also find an occasional embossed salt, but these must be deemed rare.

Peppers, or "pepper pots," as they were called, are tall (often 4″ to 5″) baluster forms with a sharp rim just below the pouring holes and a swelling lower body. Like salts, they were usually decorated with slip banding, often enhanced by Mocha.

Mustard pots, which were once found on every table at every meal, may be either cylindrical with molded foot and rim or have a bulbous lower body and long vertical neck. Tops, which always have a triangular cutout to accommodate the spoon, may be of matching yellowware or made of pewter. There is usually a handle. Though some pieces are left undecorated, most are slip-banded, and Mocha work is also seen.

Butter, too, was often found on the nineteenth-century table, though butter dishes, which were widely made in ironstone china, do not seem to have been produced in yellowware. In the collection of the East Liverpool Museum of Ceramics, however, there is a melon-shaped covered vessel with strap handle which was manufactured by the C. C. Thompson Pottery Company and termed a "citron butter jar." Since candied citron was used in fruit cakes, one would suspect that the contents were a sweetened butter or butter spread.

Cream for coffee, tea, and other use was generally kept in a squat pitcher or creamer, but more elaborate vessels might be employed for special occasions. Most popular was the cow creamer, a bovine-shaped receptacle with a hole in the back through which it was filled. Upon tilting the creamer, the cream poured through the cow's mouth. These novelty items were made primarily in Rockingham or white earthenware, but examples in yellowware have been attributed to Bennington's United States Pottery.

Miscellaneous Household Objects

Yellowware articles were long considered essential to the bedroom and bath, so a wide variety of wash bowls, soap dishes, slop jars, foot warmers, chamberpots, and bedpans may be found. As a group, these are among the less desirable of collectibles, but they were evidently among the "best sellers" of their day.

The matched pitcher and bowl (or ewer and basin, as they were known among the genteel) sets so common in white earthenware and spongeware do not appear in yellowware. Wash bowls were made by a few firms, including East Liverpool's Phoenix Pottery, which advertised 11″ and 12″ sizes during the mid-1860s. No doubt these were often combined with a suitable pitcher.

Soap dishes, called soap drainers since they had holes in the surface to allow water to pass off, were made in several shapes: round, oblong, and even in the form of a covered bowl. The C. C. Thompson Company of East Liverpool was offering soap drainers in three sizes in 1886.

Slop jars, later called combinettes, were used to dispose of waste wash water. Examples in what was termed the "Washington shape" (an odd way to commemorate our nation's father!) were on an 1850s price list of the Swan Hill Pottery. Apparently, few were made, for the form is today extremely uncommon in yellowware.

In the days before central heating, hot water bottles were deemed an essential not only in the home but also in carriages and in churches, which were rarely heated at all. Yellowware examples are found in two forms: a curving wedge or right-angle shape, with brackets to secure a wire bail handle, and a loaf-shaped form with a knob at each end. Both types have plugged holes through which they can be filled with hot water.

Chamberpots, or "chambers," as they were discreetly termed, were equally important to the well-ordered household. Almost every pottery made them from the earliest to the latest; and they will be found undecorated, slip-banded, Mocha-decorated, and embossed. They were sold both with and without matching covers, inclusion of the cover increasing the wholesale price 50 percent.

Yellowware bedpans are surprisingly common, reflecting no doubt the frequent illnesses that occurred in most families prior to the advent of modern medicine, as well as the fact that during the nineteenth and early twentieth centuries even the seriously ill were often treated at home. Two basic forms are found: the shovel-shaped or "French style," and the round. Many firms made both styles, as was the case with the Vodrey Pottery of East Liverpool which, in 1864, offered French pans at $7.00 per dozen and round at a dollar less.

Another rather unpleasant necessity was the cuspidor or spittoon. Somewhat uncommon in yellowware, though often found in Rockingham and stoneware, these seldom appear in price lists. Both octagonal and round forms are seen, as well as examples with embossed floral or geometric decoration. All examples have a top with sides sloping down to a central hole. The open turnip-shaped cuspidor does not seem to appear in yellowware. Marked specimens are very rare, though Salt & Mear of East Liverpool did make some.

Miniatures and Novelty Items

Certain yellowware miniatures were extremely popular in their day, and all remain popular collectibles. Chief among such pieces is the chamberpot. Referred to as "toy chambers," they were often a production item being offered at one dollar per dozen in the 1880s by C. C.

Thompson & Company. Though sometimes undecorated, these miniatures were usually slip-banded or Mocha-adorned.

Other less common miniatures included pitchers both plain and embossed, tiny cylindrical jugs no more than 2″ high, similar crocks, cups, and saucers and, most desirable of all, bowl and pitcher sets. The last were generally decorated in Mocha and are extremely hard to find.

All of these pieces were made sparingly, usually to order, and with the exception of the jugs and crocks known to have been made by Bennington's United States Pottery, they cannot normally be identified.

Yellowware manufacturers also turned out novelty items, many of which resembled the mantelpiece figures produced in such quantity by the kilns of Staffordshire. Bennington turned out Toby snuff jars in the form of a squatting figure whose hat could be removed to reveal the storage well. At least one of these pieces, in the collection of the Bennington Museum, bears the 1849 Lyman, Fenton & Company mark. Larger and more spectacular are a

pair of mantel ornaments in the form of poodles. More than a foot long, these were also made at Bennington. The form appears in an 1852 price list where it is offered at $13.00 per dozen wholesale, a not inconsiderable price for the day.

Smaller animals include banks in the form of reclining dogs or lions. There are also a few human figures, including an 8″ bottle in the form of a man with a fiddle and battered fedora and a mug in the shape of a man's head. None of these can be considered common.

Other Miscellaneous Forms

Yellowware potters attempted many different objects, some of which were probably quite unsuccessful, at least in terms of sales, for they were made in limited quantity and are now rarely seen. Several of these items had to do with drinking and the storage of liquids.

Both flasks and kegs or rundlets were made in the yellow clay. A flattened oval flask bearing the embossed representation of an eagle on one side and a flower on the other is the only known representative of this form in yellowware. Ramsay in *American Potters and Pottery* illustrates an identical form in Rockingham, which he attributes to East Liverpool.

Barrel-shaped kegs were used to carry water as well as stronger liquids. Smaller versions stood upright; larger ones rested on a flattened side. Both had a rimmed spout through which the liquid flowed. These too are rare and unidentified as to maker. Another novel drinking accoutrement was the flask in the shape of a book. These were made in some variety at Bennington and in Ohio and New Jersey; but the great majority found are in Rockingham, scroddle, or white earthenware. An example in yellowware from William Young & Company of Trenton may be unique.

Snuff jars and humidors are sometimes found in yellowware. Most were made in England, but quite a few were produced here also. The snuff jar is a cylindrical vessel with wide mouth in which snuff was shipped and stored. These were manufactured by several East Liverpool firms, including the Phoenix Pottery works, which listed them in an 1865 price list. Humidors, which were referred to as "tobacco jars," were intended for the temporary home storage of loose tobacco. Most were squat cylinders with domed tops. They resembled crocks, but were generally more elaborately decorated. John Patterson & Sons of Wellsville, Ohio, advertised banded humidors with matching lids in the 1880s. Slip banding, Mocha work, and embossing may all be found on humidors, and most are about a quart in capacity. Snuff jars, on the other hand, are undecorated and found in three sizes.

Among other less common yellowware examples are flowerpots, jardinieres, vases, and small ceramic baskets, also probably intended to hold small bouquets. Though advertised by John Goodwin of Liverpool as early as 1850 (they came in two sizes selling for one and two dollars per dozen respectively) and often made thereafter, yellowware flowerpots are surprisingly hard to come by. Known examples are either in the usual round, tapered form or in a less customary geometric shape.

Flower vases are usually in Art Nouveau or Art Deco form and date to the twentieth century, the majority from 1920 to 1940. Less often seen are large jardinieres. These may be as much as three feet high, and may have fluted sides and embossed floral decoration. It is also possible that they may have served as umbrella stands. Other forms include bulbous vases with holes in the sides which were used for growing onions or bulbs. In Pennsylvania, they were known as *Bolle-Kessi* or bulb kettles. For the display of smaller flowers, there were molded vessels in the shape of baskets, usually no more than 4″ or 5″ long. Most show simple embossed designs.

Other rare forms include washboards, candlesticks, and bird baths. Yellowware washboards are similar to examples found in Rockingham and spongeware but much less common. They were not advertised, and most were probably made in Ohio and Vermont. Candlesticks are scarcely ever seen. Known examples are in the turned-baluster shape and modeled on pewter forms. Bird baths are rarest of all since no examples are presently known. This is odd as several manufacturers, including John Goodwin & Sons, the Star

Pottery, and Agner & Gaston's American Pottery Works, all of East Liverpool, advertised the form.

One more yellowware form, though not really a collectible item, remains to be described: the stove tube. These pipelike objects (erroneously referred to in one text as "stove tubs") were placed in the chimney hole to receive the stove pipe. They served as insulators to prevent fires, and were made in stoneware and redware as well as yellowware.

This completes the list of known yellowware forms, yet the variety is so great that there are certainly other types in the field just waiting to be discovered. The thrill of such a find is one of the most satisfying aspects of collecting.

Advertising Pieces

Advertisers' messages are frequently found stenciled on yellowware, especially on the pie plates, bowls, jars, pitchers, and custard cups manufactured during the 1920s, 1930s, and 1940s by the Red Wing Union Stoneware Company and its successor, Red Wing Potteries. Since Red Wing was both the major producer of such pieces and also customarily decorated its yellowware with a wide white slip band between two narrower brown ones, the combination of these elements is almost a guarantee of Red Wing origin even in an unmarked example.

It does not appear that advertising on yellowware was employed in the nineteenth century, and most pieces of this nature seem to date after 1910. The merchants and manufacturers whose blurbs adorn yellowware are almost always located in the Mid- or Far West. Eastern specimens are uncommon.

Yellowware

1. Among the most common and also most desirable of mixing bowls, these banded vessels may be found in up to ten different sizes, ranging from 4″ to 14″ in diameter. Larger examples are hardest to acquire. Made in New Jersey and Ohio, c. 1880–1930.

2. Domed, covered casserole, Ohio or Minnesota, c. 1930–45. A late but uncommon piece with the appealing lines and strong color so attractive to collectors. It is 10″ in diameter.

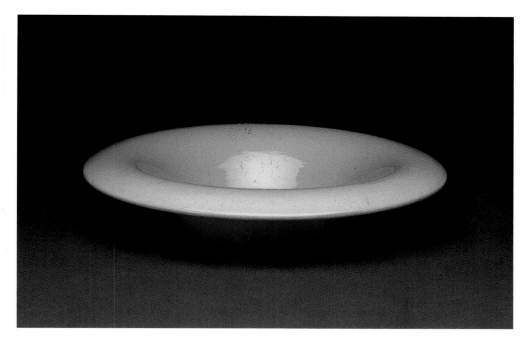

3. This unusual vessel with wide, rolled rim was probably used for floral displays. New Jersey, c. 1920–40.

4. A large mixing bowl, 11″ in diameter, with embossed floral pattern; Ohio, c. 1900–20. Referred to in catalogues as "pressed, embossed bowls," these pieces bore raised floral, geometric, or pictorial designs.

5. Both the 8″ bowl at left and the "lipped" or batter bowl on the right, which is 9.5″ across, are Mocha-decorated and date to about 1870–1900. While most Mocha was probably English, quite a few American firms also produced it. The heavy bodies and simple design seen here make it likely that these pieces are from Ohio.

6. Two colanders: left, 10″ in diameter; right, 8″. Both are c. 1870–1910 and attributed to Pennsylvania or Ohio. The two holes near the rim receive a string or wire from which the vessel is hung. Note the interesting drain-hole pattern on the piece at left.

7. A group of small cooking or serving bowls, all of which show some embossed decoration. Diameters are left to right: 8″, 4.5″, and 5″. The largest vessel is attributed to the Red Wing, Minnesota, pottery, c. 1920–40, while the others were probably made by the Morton (Illinois) Pottery Company, which referred to them as "baking nappies" in a 1920s catalogue.

8. This nest of nine nappies ranges in diameter from 4″ to 13″ and would date from 1850 to 1900. Nappies were too widely made to localize in most cases. New Jersey, Pennsylvania, Maryland, and Ohio have all yielded marked examples. Look for shallow "feet" in the form of hearts, florets, triangles, or demilunes.

9. Though uncharacteristically deep, this vessel with flaring sides and rolled rim is maybe a milk pan, as essentially similar pieces are so labeled in an 1880s catalogue of the Thompson Pottery Company of East Liverpool. It is 11″ in diameter. The form is uncommon.

10. *Below:* This large rectangular baking dish on the left bears the mark of the American Pottery Company, Jersey City, New Jersey, dating it to around 1833–45. The piece measures 8.5″ by 12″. The dish on the right measures 5″ × 9″. Yellowware of this age is rare. Most pieces date from 1880 until well into the 20th century.

11. The lipped and handled bowl at right resembles a pitcher and is extremely unusual. It is 9″ in diameter and was made in Ohio or Illinois, c. 1920–35. The small embossed lipped bowl at left is only 6.5″ in diameter and is probably from Ohio, c. 1900–20.

12. Straight-sided pitchers such as these resemble similar ones made in ironstone china. They range in height from 5″ to 9″. The largest example was made by the Morton (Illinois) Pottery Company, c. 1920–30. The one at left is attributed to the Weller Pottery Company of Zanesville, Ohio, c. 1920–35; the other two are from New Jersey or Ohio, c. 1870–1900.

13. These unusual milk pitchers date to around 1910–30 and were made in Ohio or Illinois. They are 6″, 4″, and 7.5″ high, respectively. The slip-decorated embossed pattern is uncommon.

14. Pitchers were among the most lavishly decorated yellowware. Here embossing takes the form of wood grain, walnut shell, and basketweave. The vessels are 8″, 7.5″, and 9″ tall, and were produced in Ohio or Illinois, c. 1910–40.

15. Bulbous-bodied pitchers have been made since the 18th century. These late examples date from 1900 to 1940, and range in height from 5″ to 9″. The two at right bear the mark of Zanesville's Weller Pottery. The others are from Ohio or New Jersey.

16. The finely turned Mocha pitcher at left is probably English, c. 1860–1900, and is decorated with a floral or seaweed motif. It is 8″ high. The 8.5″ diameter bowl is attributed to Ohio, c. 1870–90; and the miniature or toy chamberpot is English or Ohio, c. 1880–1915. It is only 3″ high.

17. Preserve jars were made in several different forms, including the interesting barrel shape at left. Second from left is a rare marked jar by Edwin Bennett of Baltimore, Maryland, c. 1858–65. The other pieces are from Ohio or Pennsylvania, c. 1870–90.

18. Storage crocks come in various shapes and decorations. The examples shown here vary from 4″ to 9″ in height. All were manufactured between 1900 and 1930 in Ohio or Illinois.

19. These two Mocha-decorated crocks are both English, c. 1860–90. The handled vessel with earthworm design is 7″ in diameter, while the covered example is 5.5″ wide. The original matching cover greatly enhances the value of the latter piece.

20. *Opposite:* Large covered crocks or cookie jars with embossed decoration are a late and fairly common form. This one is 10″ high and was made in New Jersey or Ohio, c. 1935–50.

21. The 6″ diameter crock at left is English, c. 1880–1910, with characteristically elaborate handles. The top is missing. In the center is a small eating bowl, 5.5″ in diameter, attributed to the Morton (Illinois) Pottery Company, c. 1910–30. The rare keeler at right is from Ohio or Illinois, c. 1890–1910. It is 8″ across.

22. The piece at left resembles a common oval baker, but the divider makes it clear that it was a serving piece. This very uncommon example is from New Jersey or Ohio, c. 1860–90. At right is an embossed and faceted serving dish, New Jersey or Ohio, c. 1910–30. It is 7″ across. The divided dish is 9″ long.

23. At left is a marked oval baker by J. E. Jeffords & Company of Philadelphia, c. 1870–75. It is 10″ long. The 8″ baker in the foreground is unmarked, c. 1870–90, and from Pennsylvania or New Jersey. At right is a rare scalloped serving dish with embossed decoration, New Jersey or Ohio, c. 1880–1900. It is 10.5″ long.

24. The beaker-form vessels seen here are 6.5″ and 4″ tall, respectively. Since they were covered, they were probably for storage or cooking, though the exact use is unknown. Ohio or Pennsylvania, c. 1870–1910.

26. *Opposite top:* Molds come in many shapes and sizes. Left to right: a fluted Turk's head, 7″ across; a common octagonal grape pattern mold, 8.5″ long; and a rare oval rabbit mold, 8″ long. All are c. 1880–1920 and attributed to Ohio or Maryland.

27. *Opposite bottom:* Miniature molds such as these 2.5″ to 4″ examples often bear the stamped mark: YELLOW ROCK, PHILA. While the manufactory has not yet been identified, the pieces were probably candy molds dating to c. 1900–30.

25. Custard cups are common, interesting, and come in a variety of decoration. Examples shown here are 3″ to 4″ tall and date c. 1880–1930. The two on the right are probably Weller of Zanesville, Ohio; but custards were so widely made as to largely preclude specific identification.

28. Associated with the kitchen are pieces such as the marked Globe Pottery (East Liverpool, Ohio) pitcher, 8″ high and c. 1885–1900; the marked Roycroft Industries (East Aurora, New York) honey pot, 5″ high, c. 1900–15; the 15″ long rolling pin, Ohio, c. 1890–1920; and the rare fruit jar funnel. The last piece is attributed to the D. E. McNichol Company of East Liverpool, c. 1895–1920, and is 4.5″ across the mouth.

29. Among the more common of yellowware, pie plates vary in size. These are 8″, 9″, and 11″ in diameter. Widely made, they can only be generally attributed to New Jersey, Pennsylvania, or Ohio. Later examples with fluted sides were made at the Red Wing, Minnesota, pottery. These pieces date to around 1870–1900.

30. Heavy, lipped, and often covered pipkins were used for cooking. The handle was often hollow to allow for steam escape. This early example is 6″ high and attributed to New Jersey or Pennsylvania, c. 1880–1900.

31. Condiment sets such as this one are hard to assemble. There were usually four to six of the 5″ spice jars, plus three larger storage crocks (here 9″ high). All were made in Illinois or Ohio, c. 1890–1920. Value is much diminished by loss of matching tops.

32. Later condiment sets often included matching pitchers, sugar bowls, and the like. This partial set is attributed to Red Wing, Minnesota, c. 1925–45.

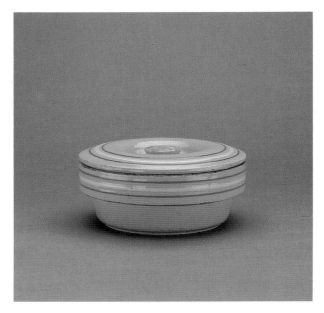

33. This charming covered serving bowl is 7″ in diameter and 4″ high. The decorative banding matches that of many bowls and pitchers. Ohio or Minnesota, c. 1910–30.

34. Mugs can be found in enough different decorative patterns to allow for an interesting collection of these alone. The ones shown here range in height from 4″ to 6″. They are all from England or Ohio, c. 1880–1910.

35. This charming diminutive Mocha-decorated teapot is English, dating from 1860–90. It is only 4″ high and 6.5″ across. The body is lathe-turned and coggle-decorated.

36. Decorated with basketweave embossing, this teapot is attributed to the C. C. Thompson pottery of East Liverpool, Ohio, c. 1890–1915. It was offered as a premium to promote Windsor Baking Powder. The pot is 7″ high and 9″ across.

37. These two mugs reflect the differences often found between English and American yellowware. The thin-walled, finely turned, and sharply decorated example at left is from England, c. 1890–1910. The American mug is heavier and the decorative figures lack clarity. It was made in Minnesota or Illinois, c. 1920–40. Height: left, 6″; right, 7″.

38. *Below:* True eating plates in yellowware are much less common than pie plates. At left is an example with scalloped edge and embossed scenes of the American West. Despite the local flavor, such pieces are believed to have been made in England for the American market c. 1915–30. The rare plate on the right is attributed to New Jersey, c. 1855–75. Diameter: both 7″.

39. Though advertised by New Jersey's Swan Hill Pottery in the 1850s, mustard pots were seldom made in this country. The three examples shown here are all English, c. 1870–1900. Each is about 4″ tall.

40. Open salts and pepper shakers or casters are uncommon and desirable. The salts at left are 3″ high, while the peppers are 4″ to 5″ tall. All are English, c. 1870–1910. Mocha or banded decoration is the rule on such pieces. Plain examples are unusual.

41. Though often seen in Rockingham, yellowware cow-form creamers are extraordinarily rare. This 6″ long example is from the United States Pottery at Bennington, Vermont, c. 1849–58.

42. Small barrels or rundlets such as these were used to carry whiskey and other liquids. The example at left is 10.5″ long, while the small barrel on the right, which is covered with dripped brown slip, is 6″ tall. Left, New Jersey or Pennsylvania, c. 1850–70; right, New Jersey, c. 1840–60.

43. Candlesticks or holders are almost unheard of in yellowware. This small stick is 3″ high and 4.5″ in diameter. It is attributed to Pennsylvania or New Jersey, c. 1850–75.

44. This extremely rare pocket flask embossed with the American eagle is attributed to East Liverpool, Ohio, c. 1840–50. An identical example in a Rockingham glaze is known. The decoration reflects the patriotism common in the 19th century. The flask is 8″ high.

45. On the left a rare soap dish attributed to Knowles, Taylor & Knowles of East Liverpool, Ohio, c. 1860–90. It is 4.5″ in diameter. On the right is a porringer cup, 3.5″ in diameter, from New Jersey or Pennsylvania, c. 1850–70.

46. Chamberpots were a standard item at all yellowware kilns. The full-size example is 10″ in diameter, while the toy potties are 2.5″ and 3″ across, respectively. Toy chambers were so popular that they were advertised by some potteries. All are from Ohio or New Jersey, c. 1880–1920.

47. One of the less popular yellowware forms, this so-called French style
bedpan is nearly 17″ long. It was made in New Jersey or Ohio, c. 1870–1910.
Another type is donut-shaped.

48. Foot warmers came in two shapes.
The pie-shaped type seen here is
attributed to New Jersey or Ohio, c. 1870–
1900; while a round or sausage form is
somewhat later, having been made from
the 1880s until well into this century. The
piece shown measures 12″ across by 7″
high.

49. Though advertised by most 19th-century manufacturers, yellowware cuspidors are not particularly common. The octagonal one at left is attributed to the Bennetts of East Liverpool, Ohio, c. 1841–44. It is 8″ across. The fluted and embossed example is from New Jersey or Ohio, c. 1870–1900, and is 8″ in diameter.

50. Yellowware banks are a real find. The barrel-shaped one at left is 4″ high, while the possibly unique pear-shaped form is 5″ tall. Both were produced in New Jersey or Pennsylvania, c. 1860–90. These pieces are much more often seen in redware or stoneware.

51. Miniatures were made as toys for children, novelties, and possibly as salesmen's samples. The plate is 3.5″ in diameter, the tiny skillet 2.5″ across, and the bean pot 3.5″ high. All are attributed to Ohio or New Jersey, c. 1870–1910.

52. Given away as premiums or as containers in which products were sold, advertising pieces were made in large numbers during the early 20th century. The bowl, 7″ in diameter, the covered crock, 5″ high, and the jar, 6.5″ tall, are all attributed to Minnesota, c. 1920–50.

55. This group of Continental European yellowware includes a piece marked "A. Tschinkel" and two others impressed "A. T." Dating from the early 20th century, these pieces are thought to be French. Such ornate ware is of little interest to most collectors.

53. *Opposite top:* Impressed marks are most common on earlier pieces. This is the mark of the American Pottery Company, active in Jersey City, New Jersey, from 1833 to at least 1845. Among the pieces found bearing this impression are plates, pitchers, and baking dishes.

54. *Opposite bottom:* Impressed mark of J. E. Jeffords & Co. on the base of an oval baker. Jeffords' Philadelphia City Pottery was established in 1868. On later pieces of yellowware the mark is ink-stamped. A marked piece is always more valuable.

56. This interesting pitcher and mug set was made by the Morton (Illinois) Pottery Company, c. 1925–35. The set was given away as an advertising premium.

57. Included in this group of bakeware is a rolling pin, colander, Turk's Head mold, mixing bowl, pie plate, pitcher, small baking nappy or custard, and an unusual paneled custard cup in the Gothic Revival style. All pieces date to the late 19th or early 20th century.

58. Canning supplies included cylindrical preserve jars such as this one impressed "Robert Arthur's Patent, Philadelphia 1855," and the uncommon sponge-decorated preserve jar funnel attributed to the McCoy Pottery Company, Roseville, Ohio, c. 1915–25. The jar is 6.5″ high and the funnel 4″ in diameter.

59. Large pieces such as this 33″ tall umbrella stand are uncommon in yellowware. It was made in New Jersey, c. 1930–45.

60. *Opposite top:* Yellowware like this would have been in use on the 19th-century farm. Pictured are a straight-sided jug, two large nappies, and a cream jar, a form common in stoneware and redware but rarely seen in yellowware. All are late 19th century except the jug, which is prior to 1925.

61. *Opposite bottom:* Highlighting this table setting is a hard-to-find coffeepot attributed to New Jersey or Ohio, c. 1920–40. It is 10″ high. Yellowware manufacturers produced everything for the kitchen and for the breakfast table as well.

62. A collection of yellowware often looks its best when displayed, as here, in an early pine cupboard. The unusual banded pitcher on the top shelf is English, c. 1900–20, and the Art Deco vase with paneled sides on the middle shelf is from New Jersey, c. 1925–35.

Spongeware Manufacturers

The collector who wishes to determine the source of his or her spongeware soon discovers a curious anomaly: while there are many forms and a variety of decoration, there are few marks. Moreover, unlike the case with yellowware, there are few catalogues, price lists, or other written materials to shed light on the field. There are several reasons for this mystery as to where American spongeware was made. In the first place, because the sponging may be done on any of several bodies—stoneware, yellowware, or white earthenware—producers tended to describe their wares not as "spongeware" but as stoneware, yellowware, or white earthenware. Thus, a manufacturer of ironstone china might decorate his wares by hand painting, transfer, or sponging, but would advertise them only as "decorated" or even simply as "ironstone."

Another limiting factor is the relatively brief history of the field. So far, few nineteenth-century spongeware makers have come to light, and there seems little doubt that the great bulk of currently collectible ware was made after 1900.

Despite these problems, it is possible to form some idea of the manufacturing history of this ware; and, interestingly enough, it parallels yellowware in that most major producers were located either in New Jersey or the Middle West, particularly Ohio.

New Jersey

Several of the Trenton white earthenware manufacturers produced sponged wares. Among them was Henry Speeler, who founded the International Pottery Company in 1853. Around 1860 the firm began to produce ironstone, and among the marked examples are square serving dishes and plates in 8″ to 10″ sizes. These are heavily sponged in blue and are backstamped in black: INTERNATIONAL POTTERY CO./TRENTON, N.J. In 1868 this company became Henry Speeler & Sons; and in 1879 it was sold to James Carr and Edward Clark. It is thought that spongeware was made until 1888.

Similar blue-sponged plates as well as soup bowls were turned out by the Etruria Pottery while operated by Ott & Brewer from 1865 until about 1882. The body of these pieces is a good-quality white earthenware.

William Leake, who was active in Trenton from 1878 to 1887, is known to have made blue-sponged novelty pieces impressed w. l. leake. These included a paperweight in the form of a cross. Such items were not for general production and are today quite rare.

At a much later date, during the first half of the twentieth century, the Fulper Pottery at Flemington, New Jersey, manufactured an extensive line of spongeware. Founded as a stoneware kiln in 1805, Fulper began to turn out spongeware in 1910 when J. M. Stangl became ceramic engineer. Pitchers, spittoons, vases, and jardinieres were among the pieces made. Marked examples include an advertising pitcher stenciled: "Made Expressly for C. Hess/manufactured by fulper pottery co./flemington, n.j."

Following a disastrous fire in 1929, operations were transferred to a company-owned pottery in Trenton, and in 1940 the firm name was changed to the Stangl Pottery. For the past forty-five years Stangl has turned out some blue-sponged vases and jardinieres, and marked examples will be encountered. These have a white earthen body rather than the stoneware found in early Fulper pieces.

Ohio

Spongeware may well have been made in great quantity at East Liverpool, Ohio. Certainly, considering the number of potteries there that were producing yellowware and white earthenwares, the materials were to hand. Nevertheless, I know of no pottery price list from this area which specifically refers to sponged wares. On the other hand, there are several firms credited with such production.

Even James Bennett, the community's first yellowware potter, is said to have made sponged serving dishes; and there is reliable information of such examples marked bennett & brothers. If these exist, the date of operation, 1841–44, would probably be the earliest for American spongeware makers.

Another early manufacturer was the Union Pottery, founded in 1844 by Thomas Croxall, one of Bennett's former employees. Croxall started with Bennett at $2.50 a week, took over his former employer's kiln in 1844, and when this was destroyed by flood in 1852, moved into the Union Pottery building. Through several moves and many partnerships, this firm survived until 1910. Among the wares attributed to it are brown-sponged pitchers and bowls.

Burford Brothers, who opened a plant at Green Lane and East 7th Street in 1879, made cream-colored and white granite ware which was sometimes sponged in blue. Plates are most common, and the backstamp reads BURFORD BROS/ELO. The firm remained in business until it was sold for other uses in 1905.

At nearby Wellsville was the pottery of John Patterson & Sons. Opening their doors in 1883 at 12th and Anderson Avenue, the Pattersons remained active until 1917. Among wares attributed to this establishment are sponged tea cups and teapots.

At least one pottery at Akron in northeastern Ohio made sponged wares. Weeks, Cook & Weeks, known as the Weeks Pottery, and a producer of stoneware from 1882 to 1900, turned out a fair number of blue-sponged syrup jugs. Some of these were advertising pieces touting the virtues of "Grandmother's Syrup."

A better-known kiln was that of Robinson & Ransbottom at Roseville, a community in south-central Ohio a few miles south of Zanesville. For the most part this company's R.R.P. & CO./ROSEVILLE logo is found on yellowware; however, there are also blue-sponged white earthen pitchers bearing the mark.

Minnesota

In terms of the number of marked or otherwise identifiable examples, Red Wing, Minnesota, must be considered the "capital" of American spongeware. From the 1890s until well into the 1940s potteries located there poured forth tens of thousands of pieces—many marked, and others identifiable by form or history.

Least common are the wares made at the Minnesota Stoneware Company, active from 1883 until it was absorbed in 1906 by the Red Wing Union Stoneware Company. Minnesota was strictly a stoneware producer, and its sponged wares are of stoneware, usually covered before decoration with a white Bristol slip glaze. Marked examples are few but include bail-handled jugs with central spout and bulbous creamers referred to in catalogues as pipkins. Marks include MINNESOTA STONEWARE CO./ RED WING MINN and M.S. CO. As with almost all Red Wing pottery, the mark is impressed, embossed, or imprinted on the bottom of the vessel.

The chief source of Minnesota spongeware is the Red Wing Union Stoneware Company, founded in 1877 as the Red Wing Stoneware Company. Prior to 1906, when this firm was redesignated the Red Wing Union Stoneware Company (which it remained until 1936), it turned out a limited number of sponged forms. These included the ubiquitous bail-handled jugs with center spout, spittoons, covered chamberpots, covered slop jars or combinettes, and umbrella stands. A variety of spongings occur, including blue on white, brown on white, and red and blue on white. Marks found are RED WING STONEWARE CO., RWSW, RWSW CO., and RED WING CO.

As the Red Wing Union Stoneware Company, this firm greatly increased the number and variety of its sponged wares. Moreover, in the early 1930s yellow clay bodies were introduced, so that spongeware might be either stoneware- or yellowware-based.

Forms known to have been manufactured here include pitchers, both embossed and plain, panel-molded mixing bowls, covered or "cap" bowls, casseroles, baking dishes, bean pots, butter crocks with matching tops, beater jars, and small-handled jugs. Marks include RED WING SAFFRON WARE (on yellow-bodied pieces), RED WING OVEN WARE, RED WING U.S.A., and MADE IN RED WING. Sponging varies widely from the common blue or brown on white to three-color variations such as red and blue on white or brown and green on yellow.

Even more shapes are found in the so-called sponge lines, which featured a horizontal band of sponging between two solid lines of slip. Introduced as early as 1929 in stoneware and in the early 1930s in yellowware, Sponge Band featured such unusual specimens as salt and pepper shakers, fruit reamers, and refrigerator jars.

Although the firm was redesignated the Red Wing Potteries in 1936, a name retained until closing in 1967, many of these spongeware forms continued to be produced until after World War II. The later wares, though, bear a single identifying logo: RED WING U.S.A.

It should also be mentioned that Red Wing is the single largest source of advertising spongeware. There are hundreds of variations—crocks, jars, bowls, pitchers, and other forms—imprinted with the names and advertising messages of grocery, liquor, shoe, drug, and hardware stores. These were sometimes included as packaging, as with the small crocks in which cheese and butter left the creamery. In most cases, however, the ceramic vessel was a "giveaway," something that was offered to the customer either with a purchase or simply to induce him or her to visit the store.

Advertising logos generally appear on the interior bottom of a piece. However, they are found elsewhere: on the sides or fronts of pitchers, on the back support of a hanging salt, or the base of a mug. As would be anticipated from the factory's location, almost all the advertisers were located in the Midwest or northwestern states.

Illinois

A serious competitor of Red Wing in the stone and household ceramics fields was the Western Stoneware Company of Monmouth, Illinois, a gigantic combine created through the amalgamation of several earlier stoneware works. Still in business, Western during 1910–40 was the nation's largest stoneware producer. Its spongeware manufacture, however, never rivaled that of its northern competitor.

Beginning in 1906, Western turned out water coolers in blue on white, mixing bowls from 5″ to 12″ in diameter in blue and brown on white, and spittoons in blue on white. In all cases the body used was Bristol-glazed stoneware. Marks found on these pieces are: WESTERN STONEWARE CO. and WESTERN STONEWARE COMPANY/MONMOUTH ILLINOIS. Western spongeware tends to be heavier and more crude than that produced at Red Wing.

The Monmouth Pottery at Monmouth, Illinois, produced some spongeware from its inception in 1893 until it was purchased by Western in 1906. Water coolers were the main item here. Sponged in blue and ranging in size from two to ten gallons, they were sometimes marked MONMOUTH POTTERY CO./MONMOUTH, ILL. Miniature water coolers were also made. But a few inches tall, these were used in promotion and sold also as novelties. Another novelty piece, but much less common, was a covered ceramic box in the form of a hen on the nest.

Other Spongeware Makers

At present only a few other spongeware manufacturers have been identified. The Fort Dodge Stoneware Company at Fort Dodge, Iowa, turned out miniature shouldered jugs with ear handles which were sponged in blue on white. These appear to have also been promotional pieces because one is stenciled across the face: FT. DODGE STONEWARE/MANUFACTORY/FORT DODGE IOWA. Other known examples bear only the base stamp, FORT DODGE. All are rare and appear to have been produced in very limited numbers.

An important spongeware manufactory was the pottery of Edwin Bennett at Baltimore, Maryland. Founded as a yellowware kiln in 1846, this firm was making white earthenwares by 1875 and continuing well into the twentieth century. Blue-sponged pitchers and serving dishes bear several marks, including a world globe pierced by a sword with the initials EBP on the handle. This cypher was adopted in 1890 when the firm became the Edwin Bennett Pottery Company. Somewhat later pieces have a stamp consisting of a crown within a wreath, the crown being imprinted EBP CO. Examples so marked date after 1896.

Unlike most spongeware, Bennett pieces have an earthenware body, usually ironstone china. In 1985 a marked and sponge-decorated Bennett pitcher brought nearly a thousand dollars at auction, one of the highest prices ever paid for a piece of spongeware.

Though it is thought that Morrison & Carr manufactured sponge-decorated white earthenware at their New York City Pottery during the second half of the nineteenth century, the only authenticated New York State maker is Frederick Ohmann of Lyons. During the years 1897–98 he produced blue-sponged stoneware pitchers, vases, and bowls. This was a small, one-man operation, and identifiable examples are few in number.

Spongeware Forms

While the variety is not as great as that encountered in the yellowware field, spongeware collectors can look forward to filling cabinets and shelves with an interesting assortment. There are dozens of different types, and even among similar examples, variations in molded and sponged decoration greatly increase one's choices. Certain categories such as mixing bowls and toilet sets also offer the opportunity to acquire matching pieces. Bowls, in great variety, are the most common forms, but pitchers and storage pieces are readily found. At the other end of the spectrum are such hard-to-acquire items as miniatures and soda fountain mugs.

Bowls

Variations among spongeware bowls are greater than among their yellowware counterparts. Two types predominate: mixing bowls and several forms with squat profiles and heavy, banded rims. The former may closely resemble yellowware mixers; so closely in fact that some examples are nothing more than banded yellowware bowls which have been embellished with spongework. Despite this identity, such spongeware vessels are rarely found in "nests" of more than three or four. Sponging may cover the entire surface of the bowl, may be confined within a wide band, or may carefully skirt a Mocha band encircling the vessel. In most cases such pieces, mold-formed or less often thrown, lack embossed decoration. However, arches, scalloping, and even elaborate fleur-de-lis may be found.

Heavier bowls with banded rims often an inch in width were referred to in a 1935 Western Stoneware Company catalogue as "shoulder bowls." However, a squatter version varying only in height and profile was termed a "milk pan."

Both mixing and shoulder bowls varied greatly in rim conformation. These might be thickly or thinly rolled, flared, or even scalloped. Bodies presented a smooth, gently curving surface or were embellished with fluting, panels, horizontal ridges or wider banding, or a multitude of embossed floral and geometric motifs. The mixers were usually footed, but most shoulder bowls lacked a pronounced base.

Yet a third form was the tapering, footed, and covered vessel referred to in circa 1920 catalogues of the Red Wing Union Stoneware Company as a cap bowl. Apparently used primarily for storage and often offered as advertising premiums, these pieces are today usually found without their original tops. Their surfaces may be plain or may show fluting or other embossed decoration.

Related vessels are the utilitarian pieces referred to in catalogues as nappies. Ranging in diameter from 4″ to 12″, these had straight sides which tapered out from the base and could be used for baking, food preparation, and serving. Unlike their yellowware counterparts, which might be found in as many as a dozen different nesting sizes, spongeware nappies appear in only four or five size variants.

The reluctance to allow spongeware out of the kitchen and into the dining room is reflected in the limited number of serving bowls. However, these can be found. There are small, round servers with smooth or scalloped rims, and even a few oval covered dishes. Many of these are quite late, and they often show a gilded edge or "lining."

Pitchers

Spongeware pitchers are perhaps the most popular of all forms in this medium; indeed, the blue-sponged pitcher has become the hallmark of the entire field. However, there are many other variants. Tall pitchers with straight or tapering sides were referred to as "water pitchers," while smaller, rounded examples were usually termed "milk pitchers." But manufacturers were by no means consistent in their terminology; a vessel might be named not for its shape but for its decoration, as with the "tankard," which was a barrel-shaped pitcher with straplike embossing.

Pitchers might be straight-sided, taper in from the base, be almost egg-shaped, or show a pronounced lower body bulge or "hip." Rims were usually rolled, but they could be scalloped or heavily banded; while the spout could vary from a massive pourer to the tiniest of wrinkles in the rim. Handles too showed great differences. Most were of the familiar ear shape, but one will also find examples that are semicircular, nearly rectangular, or even embossed so as to resemble a bent tree limb.

While the sides of a pitcher might be plain, they were more likely to bear embossed decoration. Horizontal banding was not unusual, and raised representations of flora or fauna (or both) were almost as likely to be found. Recognizable cherries, iris, corn stalks, or cattails greatly enhance the interest in many early twentieth-century examples.

Although pitchers are easy to come by, pitcher and bowl sets are not. Large and easily broken, few have survived intact to grace the shelves of contemporary collectors. The form is typically a large bowl with flaring lip, complemented by an ovoid or "bellied" pitcher with helmet-form lip, and a large handle to assure a firm grip on a vessel which might hold a gallon of water. Though other color combinations are found, blue on white seems to have been preferred; the most desirable examples have a broad blue band about the belly.

Storage Vessels

By the time that spongeware was reaching the height of its popularity, ice boxes and even the first electric refrigerators were beginning to change America's storage habits; nevertheless, many traditional dry and liquid storage containers were made in this medium. Jugs were among the earliest of these forms and among the first to vanish.

Sponge-decorated jugs are of two types: "shoulder jugs" with vertical sides rising to a curved or tapering shoulder, and an ear-shaped handle, and the so-called bailed jug with central spout and a wire bail handle attached to two "ears" or loops of clay fixed high on the curving shoulder of the vessel. Shoulder jugs were made at several different Western potteries during the early twentieth century, but only a relative few were sponge-decorated. Bailed jugs were less common, though they were being made and marked at the Minnesota Stoneware Company circa 1883–1906.

Another liquid storage container was the water cooler or keg, which, equipped with an interior filtration system, became the health-preserving water filter. Shouldered, straight-sided, or barrel-shaped, coolers were sizable pieces ranging in capacity from two to ten gallons. Almost all were sponged in blue on a white ground, and from 1906 on, the Western Stoneware Company advertised examples that bore the stenciled phrase ICE WATER across their upper bodies. Similar examples were produced by the Monmouth, Illinois, Pottery Company, around 1893–1906. Many of the latter were of bulbous form, and contained a complex filtration and purification system which in those pre-chlorine days was claimed, at least in advertising materials, to have been proven "by repeated tests by state chemists and others who gave it unqualified endorsement . . . [as] the most efficient filter we have ever examined."

However well they may have preserved the health of those who drank from them, these forerunners of the office water fountain are today rare and highly desirable examples.

Equally hard to come by are the traditional straight-sided, covered butter crocks or pots, which were advertised around 1906–16 by the Red Wing Union Stoneware Company. The form was universal and made in vast quantities in salt or Albany Slip–glazed stone-ware, but in spongeware it was and is extremely uncommon. Most known examples are in blue on white and have heavy, molded rims. The covers, when found, are dome-shaped with a flat button-shaped knob. Ranging in size from two to six gallons, they are rarely marked.

Later related items are the kitchen storage jars which are embossed with gilded letters, SUGAR, COOKIES, BUTTER, and the like. Unlike the earlier storage vessels, these have gently tapering sides, rolled rims, and touches of gilding. They were made in sets and came with matching covers, most of which have now disappeared.

Cooking and Baking Utensils

Much spongeware was made for kitchen use, and its thick, sturdy form and durable exterior suited the role perfectly. Pie plates were produced in 6″ to 12″ diameters, primarily in a brown sponging on yellow clay which can be confused with Rockingham. In fact, though, true spongeware pie plates are less common than the early tortoise-shell glaze examples.

Much more readily obtained are custard cups. Most are quite small, less than 4″ high;

but they appear in such a variety of glazes that it would be possible to amass an interesting collection based on this shape alone. Blue on white is, of course, a great favorite; but green on cream or yellow, brown on yellow, green and brown on yellow, red and blue on white, and red on yellow are but a few of the combinations available. The basic form of a handleless cup is varied by tapering or curving sides and rims, which may be plain or rolled.

Larger and more vertical in form than custards are the beater jars that were produced in the 1930s and 1940s by the Red Wing Union Stoneware Company and its successor, Red Wing Potteries. The form seems to be unique to the Minnesota company, and it was intended for the beating of eggs and similar mixing processes. The typical form has sides which are fluted, taper out gently from the base, and terminate in a rolled rim. Bases taper in abruptly to a shallow foot.

Among the rarest of sponged cooking utensils are colanders and measuring cups. As with yellowware examples, the former are really nothing more than mixing bowls with holes punched in the sides and bottom. Brown sponging on yellow is the usual color combination on these seldom-seen pieces. Measuring cups are even harder to come by. Most known are of a pint capacity, lipped, and with embossed ridges by which to measure.

Equally hard to acquire are funnels. Known examples have wide mouths, as they were intended for packing preserve jars with such frequently canned foodstuffs as tomatoes, peaches, and plums. They have gracefully formed ear handles, and some have been found in an attractive dark green sponging on yellow. Marked colanders are sometimes found, but I know of no measuring cups or funnels which can be thus identified.

Among the largest and most varied of kitchen items are the casseroles and baking dishes used in oven and stove-top cooking. Often more than a foot in diameter and with a capacity of several quarts, they served to prepare meals for families which often numbered a half dozen or more. Among the most desirable are sponged casseroles with horizontal lift handles and matching tops. An interesting characteristic of this piece is that the knob on the top is inset to make the casserole fit more easily on a low oven shelf.

Casseroles were made by the Red Wing Union Stoneware Company during the period 1910–30, and unmarked examples from other manufacturers also appear. As with all covered vessels, the example with original lid or top is most desirable. Massive covered bowls were also used for baking. These lacked handles, had thick rims similar to those of the so-called shouldered bowls, and sharply tapering bases. Like the casseroles, they could be taken directly from the kitchen to the table, thus doubling as a serving dish.

Stew pans, or "bailed cooking crocks" as they were described in a Red Wing catalogue of 1900, were intended solely for the kitchen. They had a wire bail handle attached to two horizontal "ears." If the vessel was intended for oven use, it was termed a "meat roaster" and would lack the usual turned wooden handle that was placed at the midpoint of the wire bail. Stew pans were available both with and without matching lids, and are found in various color combinations, including blue on white, brown on white, and blue on yellow. Like most such cooking vessels, they tend to lack embossed decoration, though one example illustrated here has impressed floral patterns along the sides, an extremely unusual embellishment.

Like many bail-handled vessels, stew crocks are often found minus their handles. Loss of these was apparently frequent even when the pieces were new, because there were firms which specialized in the manufacture of replacements. The firm of G. G. Westerfield, Indianapolis, offered no less than seven types of "Safety First" handles and bails in the early 1900s.

A smaller, less often seen version of the sponge-decorated, bail-handled cooking pan had a pouring spout to facilitate removal of the contents.

More specialized were the traditional bean pots whose function in the cooking of beans which were so long a staple of the American diet is well known. Among the sponged examples are several variations of the form. Some have a single small handle, rounded body, and a matching lid with buttonlike knob. The lower portion of the body may be enhanced by curvilinear fluting, but is usually plain. Other, similar pieces will have a wire bail handle joining ears set high on the vessel's shoulder. Some but not all of these pieces will also have the usual ceramic handle. The latest type is the double-handled pot without bail. This form was being made by the Red Wing Union Stoneware Company in the 1930s and often bears the firm's mark on its base.

Similar in purpose to the bean pot is the pipkin, a rounded, spouted cooking vessel, with either an ear-shaped handle or a tubular grip that may be hollow to allow steam to escape. While pipkins in yellowware and redware customarily have the elongated lifter, those that are sponge-decorated have a simple ear-shaped handle and somewhat resemble a cream pitcher with a top. Typical are the examples made and marked, circa 1883–1906, by the Minnesota Stoneware Company of Red Wing, Minnesota.

Tablewares

Not a great deal of spongeware left the kitchen and pantry to reach the dining room, but among the items that did so are plates, mugs, and teapots. Plates in several diameters, 6″, 10″, and 12″, were among the earliest examples of sponge. Larger dinner plates, whose rims may vary from plain to scalloped to twelve-sided, are most often seen; but one will also sometimes find salad and bread and butter plates. Matching soup bowls or plates are also available. Almost all are sponged in blue-on-white earthenware bodies. Among marked examples are those bearing the pierced crown mark of Ott & Brewer of Trenton, New Jersey.

Mugs are also fairly common. The form will vary from straight or slightly convex sides with a molded base to the curvilinear profile associated with contemporary teacups. An oddity here is the so-called mush cup, an outsize vessel, often of pint capacity, which comes with its own special saucer. Mush cups were used in the serving of gruel or porridge rather than beverages. Odd mush cup saucers may be mistaken for small plates. While common mugs and cups may be found in various color combinations, mush cups seem to have been made only in blue on white.

Another unusual type is the soda fountain mug. Ranging in size from 5″ to 7″, with sides that tapered out gradually from the base, these vessels were used for serving sodas and sundaes. Since they were quite heavy when full, soda fountain mugs often have massive ear-shaped handles. Embossed decorative banding will be found at the base and just below the rim.

Sponge-decorated teapots are uncommon and generally associated with Ohio, especially the Patterson Pottery of Wellsville. Most examples are sponged in brown and of a low, bulbous shape. Handles are of the ear type, and covers resemble those used on bean pots. Since the form is a traditional one, it is often hard to date these pieces.

Serving vessels are not numerous, but various forms do exist. Most often encountered are platters. The usual type is oval and sponged in blue-on-white earthenware, something typical of almost all tablewares. Less often encountered are oblong platters with embossed designs along the sides. There are also oval serving dishes of the sort referred to by manufacturers as "bakers" when made in yellowware. Much rarer is the square serving dish or bowl with fluted sides. A known example bears the EBP CO. mark of Baltimore's Edward Bennett Pottery Company.

The gravy boat is also a choice find. Sponged in blue-on-white ironstone and with the embossed floral patterns typical of late nineteenth-century whitewares, these pieces seldom appear on the market. Much the same may be said of the covered sugar bowl. Although these bowls have been found with a matching creamer, the latter is much more often encountered alone. The typical sugar bowl has two loop handles, a semi-ovoid body, and an elaborate two-tier top.

While not strictly a tableware, the sponge-decorated fat lamp is similar to the type of lighting device often used at the table. I know of only one of these extraordinarily uncommon specimens. They are also encountered in redware, most having been produced prior to 1850. This one, in white earthenware, was almost certainly an "end of day" or potter's "whimsey" piece.

Another unlikely find is the trivet or hotplate which was used to protect the tabletop from hot serving dishes. The one shown in illustration 92 (page 124) is sponged in blue and brown and has three small protuberances or "feet" on which it rests. Trivet rims may be plain or slightly molded.

Miscellaneous Household Objects

In the days before bathrooms, each bedroom in a home was provided with a toilet set, which consisted of a large pitcher and bowl, a covered chamberpot, a slop jar, or as it was termed among the genteel, a combinette, a soap dish, and a mug or beaker. Additional items might include toothbrush holders, cylindrical "brush mugs," and hair receivers (in which a woman placed strands of hair loosened in brushing). All these items have been found in spongeware, and it is evident that they were often made in matching sets. Such were being advertised in 1926 by the Western Stoneware Company.

With the exception of the pitcher and bowl, often referred to as a ewer and basin, and regarded as especially desirable in blue on white, few of these objects are highly regarded by collectors. A complete matching set, on the other hand, would be much sought after.

Another common utilitarian piece was the cuspidor, which in spongeware was a squat, round vessel with tucked-in waist and widely flaring rim. Cuspidors in sponge, referred to in some catalogues as "mottled" ware, are almost always found in blue on white. They were made in great numbers and appear in several sizes, ranging from tiny 4″ "ladies" specials to giant hotel versions a foot in diameter. Most are today used as flowerpots, though a few have found their way to the table as soup tureens!

Among the largest spongeware pieces are umbrella stands. Often nearly three feet tall, these turned cylinders had well-molded bases and resembled miniature Grecian columns. The Red Wing Union Stoneware Company began making sponged umbrella stands in 1906, and they continued in production until the thirties.

Sponged vases and jardinieres were a much later addition. Few pre-1920 examples can be found, and most seem to date from the 1930s and 1940s. Marked examples from the Stangl Pottery of Trenton, New Jersey, are sometimes seen.

Among the rarest and most desirable spongeware forms are washboards. Though no marked examples are known, most originate in Ohio or Pennsylvania, and the presence of wire nails in the wooden frames would date them to 1890 or later. Sponging is in brown or blue on a yellow base. Sizes vary from the standard adult to a charming 6″ square board clearly intended for a child.

Miniatures and Novelty Items

Sponge-decorated miniatures were made by quite a number of potteries, including ones which did not normally produce standard-sized items in this finish. For example, the Monmouth Pottery Company turned out charming blue-sponged stoneware miniature water coolers which were given away as promotional novelties by local businesses. In fact, despite the unsubstantiated legend of the "salesman's sample" miniatures, most such pieces were made either as gifts (especially for children) or advertising pieces.

By far the most common sponged miniatures are water coolers, jugs, and cuspidors. There are two basic jug forms: the straight-sided, shouldered, ear-handled jug, such as was made between 1892 and 1906 by the Fort Dodge, Iowa, Stoneware Company; and the bailed, central spout version. With the addition of a coin slot, the latter did double duty as a bank.

But the most common banks are those made in the form of a pig with coin slot in the back. Produced both in Ohio and in England during the late nineteenth and early twentieth centuries, these come in enough sponged variations to make possible a collection devoted to them alone. Among the color combinations are blue on white, brown on yellow, red on yellow, green on yellow or white, tan on white, green and brown on yellow, and red and blue on white. The list could go on and on.

Other novelty items are much less common. The miniature whiskey keg mounted on a sledge (illustration 99, page 129) is an extremely uncommon example, as is the hen-on-nest covered bowl which was produced by the Monmouth Pottery at the turn of the century. Sponged in blue-on-white Bristol glaze, the latter was a copy of the popular pressed-glass dishes of the same period.

Advertising Pieces

A whole collecting category centers on spongeware which was made for advertisers and which bore their stenciled or printed promotional messages. Everything from bowls (a very popular item for this purpose) to miniatures was used; and the message varied from a modest name and address to the "hard sell" evident in examples such as "Rasmussen Grocery, Good Things To Eat," and "It pays to trade with Michaelson."

The earliest examples showed a relationship between the object and the message. Thus, whiskey dealers advertised on jugs, creameries on butter crocks, and so forth. By the 1930s, though, it was not uncommon to find a shoe store promotion on a pitcher or a grocer sending his message via a spittoon.

There are hundreds of different spongeware advertising pieces, and they are today the exclusive interest of many collectors. For others, though, they form but an interesting sideline to the general field.

Spongeware

63. Sponged bowls, 6″ and 7″ in diameter, probably Ohio, c. 1890–1920. Similar vessels are pictured in a catalogue issued in the 1890s by the D. E. McNichol Pottery Company of East Liverpool. However, the form was widely made. These bowls are sometimes erroneously referred to as "Rockingham," but the glaze here is clearly applied with a sponge.

64. Sponged bowls, 5″, 8″, and 4″ in diameter. The center bowl is embossed, the others banded in white. The oversponging of banded yellowware is not common and may reflect a using up of excess stock. Ohio, c. 1870–1900.

65. Bowls, 5″, 8″, and 6″ in diameter, sponged within bands; Ohio or New Jersey, c. 1870–1910. This seldom-found decoration is related to Mocha. Note the difference in body color, which reflects both firing temperature (the higher the temperature, the lighter the hue) and clay mixture.

66. Spongeware bowls: left, serving bowl with fluted sides and scalloped edge; center, shallow bowl, probably part of bowl and pitcher set; right, mixing bowl. Sizes, 6″, 12″, and 8″ diameter; all date from c. 1860–1900 and are attributed to Ohio.

67. Sponged nappies, 3″, 6″, and 4″ in diameter, Ohio, c. 1900–10. As the early nappy form lost its popularity, manufacturers added sponging to increase sales appeal.

70. Sponged pitchers: left, 5″ high; right, 8″. Both were made in New Jersey or Ohio and date to c. 1900–20. The sponging on the larger piece is in the manner sometimes referred to as "chickenwire" by collectors.

68. *Opposite top:* Left to right: 7″ sponged mixing bowl with unusual collar, 10″ baking dish, and 3″ custard cup, all Illinois or Minnesota, c. 1900–25. Much spongeware made in these states employed a stoneware body, as here, rather than the yellow clay favored in New Jersey and Ohio.

69. *Opposite bottom:* Finely sponged and banded pitcher and bowl set, probably Ohio, c. 1860–80. Patterned on similar examples in porcelain or white earthenware, these wash bowls and ewers are among the most desirable of spongeware. The pitcher is 12″ high and the bowl 13″ in diameter.

71. Sponge-decorated pitchers with embossed decoration, 8″, 9″, and 8″ tall, respectively, Ohio or Illinois, c. 1900–10. The pieces at each end were dipped in glaze, then oversponged, an extremely unusual technique.

72. Three sponge-decorated cylindrical pitchers, 8″, 10″, and 8″ high. The blue-sponged example at left is by the Red Wing, Minnesota, pottery, c. 1910–20. The two others are from Ohio or Illinois and date to the same period.

73. Sponged white earthenware pitchers, 5″, 6″, 5″ tall from left. The example at right is by the firm of Griffen, Smith & Hill, Phoenixville, Pennsylvania, c. 1882–92. Though unmarked, the other examples are also attributed to Pennsylvania, c. 1880–1910.

74. Sponge-decorated yellowware straight-sided storage jugs, Ohio or Minnesota, c. 1890–1930. Though rather ordinary looking, these late-form jugs are hard to find.

75. Left to right: sponged white earthenware vase, Stangl Pottery, Trenton, New Jersey, c. 1950–60, 10″ high; stoneware pitcher by the Robinson, Ransbottom Pottery Company, Roseville, Ohio, c. 1920–30, 9.5″ high; and stoneware harvest jug, Akron, Ohio, c. 1900–10, 7″ high. The vase and pitcher are typical of the mid-20th-century spongeware now attracting collector attention.

76. Blue sponge-decorated water cooler by the Monmouth, Illinois, Pottery Company, c. 1895–1905. Some 33″ high, this is one of the larger known examples of the medium. The stenciled maker's name is unusual; in most cases it was placed on the bottom of a vessel.

77. Sponge-decorated water cooler, 24″ high, attributed to Illinois, c. 1890–1920. Water coolers came in 2, 4, 6, 8, and 10 gallon sizes. A wooden or pewter spout was placed in the hole at the base.

114

78. Left to right: spongeware storage crock, 6″ high, Red Wing, Minnesota; bowl, 8″ in diameter; and fluted serving bowl, 6″ in diameter, both bowls attributed to Illinois or Minnesota. All pieces date to c. 1900–15.

79. Sponge-decorated mug, covered storage crock, and pie plate, all from Ohio, c. 1880–1910. The mug, which is 4″ high, is typical of pieces in transition from the earlier Rockingham finish. The covered crock, 6″ high, is unusual in that it retains its original matching top. The pie plate is 9″ in diameter.

82. Two sponged stoneware cooking crocks or stew pans, 10″ and 9″ in diameter. The example at left is missing its wire bail handle. Both date to c. 1900–30 and are attributed to Illinois or Minnesota. Note the white Bristol slip often used to line kitchen wares. It indicated cleanliness to an increasingly health-conscious society.

80. *Opposite top:* At left a sponge- and gilt-decorated covered serving dish, Ohio, c. 1910–20, 5″ high; center, mixing bowl, 8″ in diameter, Ohio, c. 1900–10; at right, sponged and gilded sugar jar, Ohio, c. 1910–30, 6″ high. Gilding was frequent on later spongeware.

81. *Opposite bottom:* Custard cups 3″ to 4″ tall and sponged in various combinations. The paneled example, third from left, was probably made at Red Wing, Minnesota; the others are unidentified. All date to around 1880–1930. Custard cups were so widely made that few can be traced to a specific locality.

83. This attractive blue-sponged covered casserole or baking dish was
probably made in Iowa or Illinois, c. 1900–10. It is 11″ in diameter and rare
both for its decoration and the presence of an intact, matching top.

84. At left a small sponged casserole 8″ in diameter and at right a bean pot 6″ high.
Both pieces were made in Ohio or Minnesota, c. 1910–40. Used for baking and
serving beans, these pots were made with two, one, or no handles.

85. Ranging in diameter from 7″ to 10″, these blue-sponged white earthenware plates were made in New Jersey, c. 1860–90. The earlier the spongeware, the more likely its base will be white clay rather than yellowware or stoneware.

86. The 9″ soup bowl at left is white earthenware, by Ott & Brewer of Trenton, New Jersey, c. 1870–85. It was referred to as "Pearl Ware" in catalogues. The shallow serving bowl 6″ in diameter and the tiny 4″ mixing bowl are both stoneware. They were made in Ohio or Illinois, c. 1910–35. Note the appealing embossed heart motif on the mixing bowl.

87. Left to right: sponged dessert plate, 7″ in diameter, New Jersey, c. 1870–90; sponged and banded ewer, 7″ high, Ohio or Illinois, c. 1890–1910; and sponged and banded cuspidor, New Jersey or Ohio, c. 1890–1920. The plate is white earthenware, the other two pieces are stoneware.

88. Cups and saucers in spongeware are uncommon. At left is a so-called mush cup with saucer 6″ in diameter. The cups at center and right are both 3″ high. All are from Pennsylvania or Ohio, c. 1870–1900; and the set at right bears the mark of Burford Brothers of East Liverpool.

89. This unusual sponged soda fountain mug was probably made in Ohio or Maryland, c. 1890–1930. Produced in limited quantities, such pieces are now hard to come by. It is 7″ high.

90. Platters in sponge decoration are rare and desirable. These examples are, from right to left, 9″, 11″, and 10″ long. The one in front has an attractive, scalloped rim. All were made in Maryland or New Jersey, c. 1870–95.

91. These interesting examples reflect the variety to be found in spongeware. Left to right: 9″ nappy; beater or serving bowl, 5″ high; and cereal bowl, 6″ in diameter. All were made in New Jersey or Pennsylvania, c. 1880–1910.

92. Another uncommon find is the trivet. The example shown here is 6″ in diameter, sponged on white earthenware. It is from Maryland or New Jersey. The teapot is 5.5″ high and attributed to the Patterson Pottery of Wellsville, Ohio, c. 1890–1915. The uncommon small-lipped stew pot is only 4″ high. It is probably from Ohio as well.

93. Sponged white earthenware. Left to right: square serving dish with scalloped edge marked by the Edwin Bennett Pottery, Baltimore, Maryland, c. 1890–1900; rectangular baker, 8″ by 10″, attributed to the International Pottery Company of Trenton, c. 1880–90; and marked Bennett oval baker or serving dish, 7″ long and dating c. 1880–1900.

94. Tablewares in sponged white earthenware, including a 7″ long gravy boat, covered sugar 6″ high, and 5″ creamer. All are from Maryland or Pennsylvania and date to c. 1870–1900. These pieces were cast in the same molds used in manufacturing contemporary ironstone china.

95. The sponged white earthenware soap dish seen at left may have been part of a toilet set. It is 3.5″ by 4″ and was made c. 1900–20. A missing top reduces the value of the c. 1890–1910 bean pot. It is 7″ high. The extremely rare fat lamp was made around 1860–80 in Pennsylvania. The other two pieces are attributed to Ohio.

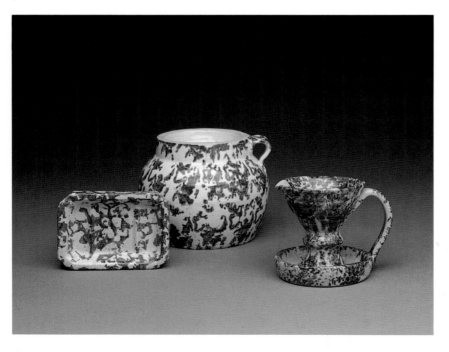

96. Sponged white earthenware vase at left is 8″ in diameter and dates c. 1900–10. The handled vase is 9″ high and was made c. 1930–40. Both are from New Jersey. Such items as vases and jardinieres are almost always 20th century.

97. A two-piece vase or plant holder attributed to the Stangl Pottery, Trenton, New Jersey, c. 1950–65. It is 10″ high. Later spongeware is inexpensive and offers opportunities for the beginning collector.

98. This brown-sponged yellowware washboard was made in Ohio, c. 1880–90. Though often thought of as much earlier, these pieces can be dated by the wire nails in the frames. Wire nails were invented in the last quarter of the 19th century. The board measures 17″ × 10″.

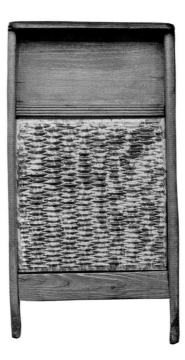

99. Sponged keg on sleigh, Ohio, c. 1900–10, 7″ long. This novel piece was used to store alcoholic beverages. Similar barrel-form miniatures are found in redware and stoneware.

100. Bank in the form of a miniature bailed jug, sponged
stoneware, 3″ tall, attributed to the Minnesota Stoneware
Company, Red Wing, Minnesota, c. 1885–1905. Miniatures are
among the most popular collectibles.

101. A group of sponged pig-form banks in stoneware, yellowware, and white earthenware, all
Ohio or English, c. 1900–20. These pieces were widely made both here and in England. They come
in sufficient variety to provide the basis for a specialized collection.

102. Two sponge-decorated bowls, 7″ and 6″ in diameter, with advertising material imprinted on the interior. These pieces were made at the Red Wing, Minnesota, pottery, c. 1920–30. Red Wing produced dozens of different advertising vessels.

103. Base of sponged pitcher showing stamped mark of the Robinson Ransbottom Pottery Company of Roseville, Ohio. Marks were more often impressed into the soft clay before firing. Freehand incising and paper labels were also used to identify spongeware.

104. This group of spongeware includes, left to right: a small 4″ high pitcher in the form often referred to as a pipkin; a shallow serving bowl, 4″ in diameter; a plate, 7″ in diameter; a 3″ high custard cup; and a large mixing bowl, 10″ across, with embossed heart design. All were made c. 1890–1930 in Minnesota or Ohio.

105. This c. 1915–30 toilet set includes, left to right: a drinking mug 4.5″ high; a waste jar or combinette, 16″ high; a soap dish, 5.5″ in diameter; and a toothbrush holder, 6″ high. The pieces are attributed to Ohio. Sets of this sort were indispensable during the 19th century and were still being advertised in the late 1920s.

106. This large sponge-decorated stoneware casserole is 11″ in diameter and was made c. 1910–25 by the Red Wing, Minnesota, pottery company. An entire meal could be cooked in such a vessel.

107. From left to right: pitcher with embossed decoration, 8″ high; cooking crock or stew pan, 9″ in diameter; bowl, 6″ in diameter; and small pitcher or pipkin, 5″ high. All were made in Ohio or Illinois, c. 1900–25.

108. The scalloped serving bowl at left is unusual. It is 6″ in diameter. The shallow wash bowl at center is a foot across and bears the interesting central-sponged motif often found in pitcher and bowl sets. Both pieces are attributed to Ohio, c. 1860–1900. The 3″ custard cup at right dates to c. 1900–10 and is also from Ohio.

109. A rare sponge-decorated white earthenware pap boat from Pennsylvania, c. 1830–50. Used to feed babies and the sick, these pieces are seldom encountered. Courtesy of Sharon W. Joel, Antiques, Jacksonville, Florida.

110. This group of pig banks is in stoneware and yellowware. Pieces are 3.5″ to 5″ in length, and all were made in Ohio or England during the period 1900–20.

111. Spongeware is readily distinguished from spatterware, several examples of which are shown here. The spatter decoration may be used alone, as in the cup and saucer at right; or combined with freehand painting, as in the coffeepot on the left, or with transfer printing, as seen in the center plate. All pieces are English, c. 1850–80.

112. Cut spongeware is related to spatter. Most pieces were produced in England, but the oval baker or serving dish and saucer shown here were made by the Mayer Pottery Company of Beaver Falls, Pennsylvania, c. 1881–85. The baker is 8″ long, the saucer 5″ in diameter.

113. Rockingham-glazed wares such as the two coachman
bottles seen here can be distinguished from spongeware by
the fact that in the former the glaze is dripped on, lacks a
pattern, and covers most of the clay body. These pieces were
made at the United States Pottery, Bennington, Vermont,
c. 1849–58. They are about 8″ tall.

APPENDIX:
A LIST OF SPONGEWARE AND
YELLOWWARE MAKERS

The following lists reflect the most current and complete record of American manufacturers of yellowware and spongeware. There is also a brief tabulation of English and Canadian makers, in most cases those whose marked wares may come to the attention of collectors.

As mentioned earlier, most of these ceramics were apparently unmarked by their makers, so few of the entries contain identifying cyphers. However, readers—especially if they are located in the vicinity of old potteries—may familiarize themselves with possible sources of marked pieces by examining these lists. As has proven to be the case with stoneware and redware, such familiarity will lead to the discovery of previously unknown marks, as well as the recognition of firms whose products have so far escaped attention.

Yellowware Manufacturers

CALIFORNIA

East Oakland
Brannon, Daniel (Pioneer Pottery)
1856–1887

Los Angeles
Pacific Clay
Manufacturing Company
1880–1930
PACIFIC

Bauer, J. A., & Company
1890–1958
BAUER

CANADA

Cape Rouge
Gauvreau, L. P. & Brother
1864–1866
CAP ROUGE POTTERY

Howison & Chartre
1860–1864

Hamilton
Campbell, Robert
1881–1899

Iberville
Pearson, Charles E.

1880–1887
C.E.P.

Quebec
Bell, William & David
1860–1870

St. Johns
Farrar, George H. & Lucius E.
1871–1878
ST. JOHNS POTTERY

Bowler, Elijah
1878–1889

CONNECTICUT

Norwalk
Day, Noah S. & George
1832

DELAWARE

Hockessin
Marshall, Abner
1859–1866

ENGLAND

Burton-on-Trent
Sharpe Brothers & Company
1838–1890
SHARP'S PATENT/WARRANTED/FIRE PROOF

Derbyshire
Greene, T. G. (Church Gresley
    Pottery)
1790–1930
T. G. GREEN/CHURCH GRESLEY; CHURCH
    GRESLEY/MADE IN ENGLAND

Woodville Potteries
1810–1895
WOODVILLE/POTTERIES

Wooden Box Pottery
1817–1905
WOODEN BOX; JOSEPH THOMPSON/
    WOODEN BOX/POTTERY/DERBYSHIRE

Woodville Pottery
1833–1925
WOODVILLE POTTERY

Rawden Pottery
1840–1886
RAWDEN POTTERY

Staley, Richard (Old Midway
    Pottery)
1880–1915
RICHARD STALEY & SONS/FIREPROOF

ILLINOIS

Morton
Morton Pottery Company
1920–1940

Peoria
Peoria Pottery Company
1859–1863

American Pottery Company
1864–1873

INDIANA

Troy
Indiana Pottery Company (Jacob
    Lewis, Samuel Casseday, James
    C. Lewis)
1836–1837

Clews, James
1837–1838

Vodrey, Jabez
1839–1846

Saunders, James,
& Wilson, Samuel
1851–1863

Hincho, Benjamin
1865–1888

KENTUCKY

Louisville
Lewis, William
1829–1839

Louisville Pottery
1920–1930

MARYLAND

Baltimore
Chesapeake Pottery
1880–1882

Bennett, Edwin & William
1846–1848
E. & W. BENNETT/CANTON ST./
    BALTIMORE

Bennett, Edwin
1848–1875
J. BENNETT'S PATENT/DEC. 2, 1858

MASSACHUSETTS

Boston
Boston Earthenware Manufactory
1854–1876

New England Pottery Company
1876–1878

MINNESOTA

Red Wing
Red Wing Union Stoneware
    Company
1933–1936
RED WING/SAFFRON/WARE

Red Wing Potteries
1936–1945
RED WING/SAFFRON/WARE

MISSOURI

Kaolin
Pyatt, George
1859–1863

Shepard, Elihu A.
1852–1865

NEW JERSEY

Elizabeth
Pruden, John
1835–1879

Jersey City
Henderson, David & James
1828–1833
D. & J. HENDERSON JERSEY CITY;
D. & J. HENDERSON/1829

American Pottery
Manufacturing Company
1833–1845
AMERICAN POTTERY/MANUFACTURING
  COMPANY/JERSEY CITY; AMERICAN/
  POTTERY CO./JERSEY CITY, N.J.

Matawan
Rue, J. L., Pottery Company
1871–1875
THE J. L. RUE POTTERY CO./MATAWAN/
  N.J.

Newark
Krumeich, Balthaser
1836–1900

Gillig, Daniel, & Company
1840–1856

Osborne, John H.
1856–1862

Perth Amboy
Eagle Pottery
1858–1865

Hall, Alfred & Sons
1866–1876

Rahway
Turner, William
1868–1870

South Amboy
Hancock, John & William
1828–1840
HANCOCK POTTER

Cadmus, Abraham
(Congress Pottery)
1849–1854
A. CADMUS/CONGRESS POTTERY/SOUTH
  AMBOY/N.J.

Swan Hill Pottery
1849–1876
SWAN HILL/POTTERY/SOUTH AMBOY

Rue, John L., & Company
1860–1871
J. L. RUE POTTERY COMPANY

Hanks, Edward, & Fish, Charles
1850–1851
HANKS & FISH/SWAN HILL/POTTERY/
S. AMBOY, N. JERSEY

Carr, James
1852–1855

Wooten, Joseph
1856–1858

Coxon, Charles
1858–1860

Sparks & Moore
1849–1850

Trenton
Taylor, James, & Speeler, Henry
1852–1872

Millington, Astbury & Young
1853–1857

Excelsior Pottery (Wm. Young)
1857–1879
W. H. YOUNG/TRENTON

Astbury & Millington
(Carrol St. Pottery)
1857–1860

Cory, I. W.
1867–1870
I. W. CORY/TRENTON

Moses, John & Sons
1860–1890

Union
Haidle & Zifph (Union Pottery)
1875–1890

Woodbridge
Salamander Works
1838–1850
SALAMANDER/WORKS/CANNON STREET/
  NEW YORK

NEW YORK

East Aurora
The Roycroft Shops
1915–1925

THE ROYCROFT SHOPS EAST AURORA
  N.Y.; initial R

Mechanicville
Lewis, Otto V.
1860
OTTO V. LEWIS/MECHANICVILLE

New York City
Carr, Thomas
(New York City Pottery)
1856–1860
CITY POTTERY/WEST 12TH ST. N.Y.

Syracuse
Farrar, William H.
1857–1868

Coykendall, Charles W., &
  Company
1868–1871

Manchester, Charles,
& Clark, F. W.
1868–1869

White, Thomas G.
1869

Tivoli
Bonnet, Stephen
1797–1798

Utica
Central New York Pottery
1890–1892

OHIO

Akron
Johnson, Whitman & Company
1857

Rowley & Baker
1850–1857

Cincinnati
Dallas, Frederick
1865–1869

OHIO (continued)

Pollock, Samuel
(Dayton St. Pottery)
1859–1874

Coultry, P. L.
1874–1900

Miller, August
1865–1900

Fisher, John (Berlin St. Pottery)
1871–1895

Mappes, H. (Vine St. Pottery)
1859–1880

Mappes Brothers
1880–1890

Kendall, Uriah & Sons
1839–1870
U. KENDALL & SONS

Scott, George
1853–1859

Scott, George & Sons
1889–1900

Lessel, Peter
1852

Brewer, Tunis
1856–1859

Eichenlaub, Valentine
1852–1857

Brewer, Tunis, & Tempest
1854–1856

Skinner, Greatbach & Company
1854–1857

Brewer, J. A.
1859–1869

Behn, Andrew
1857–1877

Tempest, Michael & Nimrod
1857–1865

Whitman, Robinson & Company
1862–1870

Tempest, Brockman & Company
1862–1867

Behn, George Peter
1857–1900

Doane, James
1831–1837

Bromley, William
1849–1860

Crooksville

Hull, A. E., Pottery Company
1905–1917
HULL

East Liverpool

Bennett, James
1840–1844
BENNETT AND BROTHERS/LIVERPOOL,
OHIO; BENNETT & BROTHERS

Croxall, Thomas & Brothers
1844–1852

Harker, Benjamin, Sr.
1840–1846

Etruria Pottery
1840–1846

Harker, Taylor & Company
1846–1851
HARKER, TAYLOR & CO/EAST
LIVERPOOL/OHIO

Harker, Thompson & Company
1851–1854

Harker, George S., & Company
1854–1879

Salt & Mear
(Mansion House Pottery)
1842–1850
SALT & MEAR

Smith, William G., & Harker,
Benjamin, Jr.
1850–1857

Foster, James, & Garner,
William G.
1857–1863

Croxall & Cartwright
1863–1888
CROXALL & CARTWRIGHT/EAST
LIVERPOOL/OHIO

Croxall, G. W. & Sons
1888–1898

Croxall Pottery Company
1898–1912

Goodwin, John
1844–1846
J. GOODWIN/1846

Baggott, S. & W. (Eagle Pottery)
1853–1890

Ball & Morris (Union Pottery)
1845–1855

McGilvary & Orr
1855–1857

Brunt, William, Sr.
1847–1852

Brunt, William, & Bloor, William
1852–1853

Brunt, William, Sr.
1853–1881

Woodward & Vodrey
1847–1848

Woodward, Vodrey & Booth
1848–1849

Woodward, Blakely & Company
1849–1857

Knowles & Harvey
1853–1867

Knowles, Isaac W.
1867–1870

Knowles, Taylor & Knowles
1870–1872

Surles & Gamble
1879–1882

Flentke, Harrison & Company
1882–1885

Vodrey & Brothers (Palissy Works)
1857–1896

Henderson, John
(Salamander Pottery)
1847–1857

Morley, Goodwin & Flentke
1857–1874

Flentke, Worcester & Company
1871–1877

Flentke, Harrison & Company
1877

Brunt, William, Jr., & Company
1859–1878

Thompson, Jobling,
Taylor & Company
1865–1867

West, Hardwick & Company
1867–1879

Manley & Cartwright
1864–1872

Manley, Cartwright & Company
1872–1880

Cartwright Brothers Company
1880–1890

Goodwin, John (Novelty Pottery)
1863–1865

Goodwin, John
1865–1869

McNicol, Burton & Company
1869–1892

McNicol, D. E., Pottery Company
1892–1930

O'Connor, Edward
1895–1902

Hill, Brunt & Company
1867–1874

McDevitt, Cochran & Company
1868–1871

Thompson & Herbert
1868–1870

Thompson, Cassius & Josiah
1868–1884
THE C. C. THOMPSON POTTERY CO./ . . .
EAST LIVERPOOL, OHIO

Starkey & Ourly (Star Pottery)
1871–1872

Worcester, Samuel & Son
1872–1876

Bulger & Worcester
1876–1886

Agner & Fouts (American Pottery)
1863–1881

Agner & Gaston
1881–1887

Foster, Joseph, & Garner, George
1857–1860

Foster, Joseph, & Rowley, James
1860–1865

Foster, Joseph, & Rigby
1865–1867

Rigby, T., & Co. (Broadway
Pottery)
1867–1872

Wyllie Brothers
1848–1854

Shenkel, Allen & Co.
(Globe Pottery)
1881–1888
THE GP CO. E.L.OH; THE GLOBE
POTTERY/EAST LIVERPOOL

Harrison, Richard, & Company
1852–1855
RICHARD HARRISON & CO./EAST
LIVERPOOL/OHIO

Fultonham
Weller, Samuel
1873–1900
WELLER

Middlebury
Raleigh, Enoch, & Baker, Herbert
1850–1852

Roseville
Robinson, Ransbottom
Pottery Company
1925–1955
R.R.P. & CO./ROSEVILLE OHIO/U.S.A.

St. Clair Township
Longs Run Pottery
1830–1852

Wellsville
Patterson, John & Sons
1882–1890

Patterson Brothers Company
1887–1917

Garner, George, & Bullock, Enoch
1845–1847

Wells, S.
1850–1852

Zanesville
Sullivan, Samuel
1808

Howson, Bernard & Company
1840–1850

Pyatt, George
1846–1879

Rambo, Joseph
1863–1870

Pyatt, George, & Getz
1851–1852

Tremont Pottery (J. G. Pyatt)
1879–1900

OHIO (continued)

Wilbur, Alfred
1873–1878

Bombaugh, Calvin
1873–1900

Hanelsack, Daniel
1874–1880

Smiley, H. K.
1878

Key & Swope
1879–1900

King, Jacob S., & Swope, John T.
1879–1910

PENNSYLVANIA

Beaver Falls
Graff, J.
1873–1880

Honey Brook
Schofield, William
1890–1900

Kennet Square
Brosius, Edwin
1870–1880

New Brighton
Elverson, Thomas
1862–1880

Smith, A. F.
1880–1900

Oxford
Beech, Samuel W.
1874–1875

Hutchinson, Fulton C. & Samuel
1869–1872

Pfeiffer's Corners
Wagner, George A.
1875–1876

Philadelphia
Allen, George
1857–1858

Jeffords, J. E., & Co.
1868–1904
FIREPROOF/J. E. JEFFORDS & CO./PHILA/
    PATENTED JUNE 28, '70

Haig, Thomas and James
1833–1858

Miller, Abraham
1840–1858

Spiegel, Isaac
1837–1860

Mullowny, John (Capt.)
1810–1816

Galloway & Graff
1868–1900

Phoenixville
Phoenixville Pottery
1867–1882

Pittsburgh
Bennett, Daniel
1849–1860

Vodrey, Jabez, & Frost,
1827–1830

Bennett, James & Brothers
1844–1849

SCOTLAND

Saracen Pottery
1875–1913
B.M. & CO./SARACEN POTTERY

VERMONT

Bennington
Fenton, C. W., & Norton, Julius
1844–1847
NORTON & FENTON/EAST BENNINGTON;
    NORTON & FENTON/BENNINGTON

Lyman, Fenton & Park
1847–1849
LYMAN, FENTON & CO./FENTONS/
    ENAMEL/PATENT/1849/BENNINGTON, VT.

United States Pottery Company
1849–1858
LYMAN, FENTON & CO./FENTONS/
    ENAMEL/PATENT/1849/BENNINGTON, VT.

WEST VIRGINIA

Newell
Larkins Bros. (Virginia Pottery)
1848–1857

Thompson, William
1857–1861

Spongeware Manufacturers

IOWA

Fort Dodge

Fort Dodge Stoneware Company
1892–1906
FORT DODGE STONEWARE CO./FORT
   DODGE, IOWA; FORT DODGE

MARYLAND

Baltimore

Bennett, Edwin, Pottery Company
1875–1910
EBP CO. or EBP; EBP CO./WARRANTED

MINNESOTA

Red Wing

Minnesota Stoneware Company
1883–1906
MADE BY MINN. S.W. CO. RED WING;
   MINN. S.W. CO.; M.S. CO.

Red Wing Stoneware Company
1877–1906
RED WING STONEWARE CO.; RWSW;
   RWSW CO.; RED WING CO.

Red Wing Union
Stoneware Company
1906–1936
RED WING OVEN WARE; RED WING
   SAFFRON WARE; RED WING, USA

Red Wing Potteries
1936–1950
RED WING U.S.A.

NEW JERSEY

Flemington

Fulper Pottery Company
1920–1929
MANUFACTURED BY FULPER POTTERY
   CO./FLEMINGTON, N.J.

Trenton

Stangl Pottery
1930–1960
HAND PAINTED/STANGL/TRENTON. N.J.
   SINCE 1805

International Pottery Company
1860–1868
INTERNATIONAL POTTERY CO./TRENTON,
   N.J.

Speeler, Henry & Sons
1868–1879

Carr, James, & Clark, Edward
1879–1888

Ott & Brewer, Etruria Pottery
1865–1882
O.B. below crown pierced
by sword

Leake, William
1878–1887
W. L. LEAKE

NEW YORK

Lyons

Ohmann, Frederick
1897–1898

OHIO

Akron

Weeks, Cook & Weeks
1882–1900

East Liverpool

Bennett, James & Brothers
1841–1844
BENNETT & BROTHERS

Croxall, Thomas (Union Pottery)
1852–1910

McNicol, D. E., Pottery Company
1892–1930

Croxall, Thomas (Union Pottery)
1852–1910

Burford Brothers
1879–1905
BURFORD BROS./E.L.O.

Roseville

Robinson, Ransbottom
Pottery Company
1925–1955
R.R.P. CO./ROSEVILLE, O./U.S.A.

McCoy Nelson Pottery Company
1910–1926
MC; MC COY

Wellsville

Patterson, John & Sons
1883–1917

PENNSYLVANIA

Phoenixville

Griffin, Smith & Hill
1882–1902

BIBLIOGRAPHY

There are a substantial number of books, articles, and exhibition catalogues which touch upon or deal extensively with the fields of yellowware and spongeware. This bibliography is selective in the sense that it lists only those works which discuss the field in some depth and which are, in most cases, readily available to the reader.

Barber, Edwin Atlee, *Catalogue of American Potteries and Porcelains*. Philadelphia: The Pennsylvania Museum, 1893.

——, *Marks of American Potters*. Philadelphia: Patterson & White Co., 1904; repr., Southampton, N.Y.: Cracker Barrel Press, 1972.

——, *The Pottery and Porcelain of the United States: An Historical Review of American Ceramic Art from the Earliest Times to the Present Days*. New York and London: G. P. Putnam's Sons, 1893: combined with *Marks of American Potters* and reprinted, New York: Feingold & Lewis, 1976.

Barret, Richard C., *Bennington Pottery and Porcelain*. New York: Bonanza Books, 1958.

Blacker, J. F., *Collecting Old English Pottery*. Toronto, Canada; Coles Publishing Co., 1980.

Clement, Arthur W., *Our Pioneer Potters*. York, Pa.: The Maple Press Co., 1947.

Collard, Elizabeth, *Nineteenth Century Pottery and Porcelain in Canada*. 2nd ed., Kingston and Montreal; McGill-Queensbury University Press, 1984.

De Groot, T. Krista, "Of Rings and Brooches and Mugs and Jugs," *Antiques and the Arts Weekly*, April 18, 1986.

Denker, Ellen and Bert, *The Warners Collector's Guide to North American Pottery and Porcelain*. Clinton, N.J.: The Main Street Press, 1982.

De Pasquale, Dan and Gail, and Peterson, Larry, *Red Wing Collectibles*. Paducah, Ky.: Collector Books, 1985.

——, *Red Wing Stoneware*, Paducah, Ky.: Collector Books, 1985.

Early Arts of New Jersey—The Potter's Craft, c. 1600–1900, exhibition catalogue. Trenton, N.J.: State Museum Department of Education, 1956.

Foshee, Rufus, "If it Doesn't Have a Peafowl or a Tulip," *Maine Antiques Digest*, December 1978.

Gallo, John, *Nineteenth and Twentieth Century Yellowware*. Richfield Springs, N.Y.: Heritage Press, 1985.

Gates, William C., Jr., and Ormerod, Dana C., "East Liverpool, Ohio, Pottery District, Identification of Manufacturers and Marks," *Historical Archaeology*, Vol. 16 (1–2),

The Society for Historical Archaeology, 1982.

Godden, Geoffrey, *British Pottery and Porcelain, 1780–1850*. New York: A. S. Barnes, 1963.

Greaser, Arlene and Paul H., *Homespun Ceramics—A Study of Spatterware*. Allentown, Pa.: privately printed, 3rd ed., 1967.

James, Arthur E., *The Potters and Potteries of Chester County, Pennsylvania*. West Chester, Pa.: Chester County Historical Society, 1945; rev. edn., Exton, Pa.: Schiffer Publishing, 1978.

Ketchum, William C., Jr., *Pottery and Porcelain: The Knopf Collectors' Guides to American Antiques*. New York: Alfred A. Knopf, 1983.

——, *The Pottery and Porcelain Collector's Handbook*. New York: Funk & Wagnalls, 1971.

Leibowitz, Joan, *Yellowware—The Transitional Ceramic*. Exton, Pa.: Schiffer Publishing, 1985.

Lewis, Griselda, *The Collector's History of English Pottery*. New York: The Viking Press, 1969.

Martin, Jim, and Cooper, Bette, *Monmouth—Western Stoneware*. Des Moines, Iowa: Wallace-Homestead Book Co., 1983.

Myers, Susan, *Handicraft to Industry: Philadelphia Ceramics in the First Half of the Nineteenth Century*. Washington, D.C.: Smithsonian Institution Press, 1980.

New Jersey Pottery to 1840, exhibition catalogue. Trenton, N.J.: New Jersey State Museum, 1972.

The Pottery and Porcelain of New Jersey Prior to 1876, exhibition catalogue. Newark, N.J.: The Newark Museum Association, 1915.

The Pottery and Porcelain of New Jersey, 1688–1900, exhibition catalogue. Newark, N.J.: The Newark Museum, 1947.

Ramsay, John, *American Potters and Pottery*. Boston: Hale, Cushman & Flint, 1939; repr., New York: Tudor Publishing Co., 1947.

Robacker, Earl F. and Ada F., *Spatterware and Sponge: Hardy Perennials of Ceramics*. South Brunswick and New York: A. S. Barnes, 1978.

Schwartz, Marvin D., *Collector's Guide to Antique American Ceramics*. Garden City, N.Y.: Doubleday, 1969.

Spargo, John, *Early American Pottery and China*. New York: The Century Company, 1926; repr., Rutland, Vt.: Charles E. Tuttle Co., 1974.

Stradling, J. G., "East Liverpool, Ohio: an American pottery town," *The Magazine of Antiques*, June 1982.

Watkins, Lura W., *Early New England Potters and Their Wares*, Cambridge, Mass.: Harvard University Press, 1950; repr., Hamden, Conn.: Archon Books, 1968.

A NOTE ON THE TYPE

The text of this book was set in a digitized version of Cheltenham Light, designed by the architect Bertram Grosvenor Goodhue in collaboration with Ingalls Kimball of The Cheltenham Press of New York. Cheltenham was introduced in the early twentieth century, a period of remarkable achievement in type design. The idea of creating a "family" of types by making variations on the basic type design was originated by Goodhue and Kimball in the design of the Cheltenham series.

The display was set in Cheltenham Bold and Cheltenham Book, utilizing the variations available in this face.

Composition by The Sarabande Press, New York, New York.
Color separations, printing, and binding by
Toppan Printing Company, Tokyo, Japan.
Endpaper pattern created by Claire Maziarczyk.
Designed by Virginia Tan.

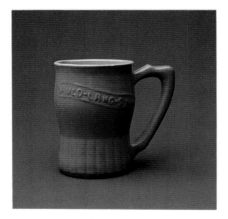